Hawley Families in America:

Descendants of Benjamin Hawley of Chester County, Pennsylvania

The Society of the Hawley Family, Inc.

The Society of the Hawley Family would like to acknowledge the compiler of this book, Raymond G. Hawley. We are grateful to Raymond for years of coordinating the flow and input of information. Thank you for a job well done.

The Society of the Hawley Family recognizes Charles W. Hawley and Dorothy M. Hawley, immediate past president and recorder. We are thankful for their decades of service to our members. They truly exemplify the spirit of The Society of the Hawley Family. Thank you for all you have done.

HERITAGE BOOKS
2025

HERITAGE BOOKS

AN IMPRINT OF HERITAGE BOOKS, INC.

Books, CDs, and more—Worldwide

For our listing of thousands of titles see our website at
www.HeritageBooks.com

Published 2025 by
HERITAGE BOOKS, INC.
Publishing Division
5810 Ruatan Street
Berwyn Heights, Md. 20740

Heritage Books by the author:

Hawley Families in America: Descendants of Benjamin Hawley of Chester County, Pennsylvania

Hawley Families in America: Descendants of Peter Hawley of Montgomery County, Virginia

International Standard Book Numbers
Paperbound: 978-0-7884-0629-4

SUIVEZ MOI.

𝕳𝖆𝖜𝖑𝖊𝖞.

A color print of the Hawley coat-of-arms is available from
The Society of The Hawley Family, Inc.
Box 444, Stratford, CT 06497

TABLE OF CONTENTS

PREFACE

Every effort has been made to produce an easy to use and easy to read genealogy. The type is fairly large; every descendant has a complete record; every record has references indicating where each event was found; and blank spaces have been provided for missing spouses and spouse parents.

There are 243 descendants and 110 spouses.

We request that any corrections and/or additions be sent to:

> The Society of The Hawley Family, Inc.
> Box 444
> Stratford, CT 06479

This book and DESCENDANTS OF PETER HAWLEY of Montgomery, Virginia were published simultaneously.

Two books yet to come and also to be published simultaneously are:

DESCENDANTS OF JOSEPH HAWLEY of Stratford, CT

DESCENDANTS OF THOMAS HAWLEY of Roxbury, MA
   brother of Joseph

One other book being planned is:

SMALL UNCONNECTED HAWLEY FAMILIES, COUPLES AND LONERS

                                                     R G H

"WHAT'S IN A NAME?"

I remember very well, when quite a lad, having speculated, as doubtless most children do, as to why one man was called HAWLEY and another SMITH. The question "How came the first man who was called Hawley, to be so called?" was one of profound import, and one which I cannot now answer, of course, any more certainly than in boyhood. It may be harmless if not satisfactory to say, that when this inquiry was quite a new one comparatively, I supposed and hoped that the name was of Saxon origin. This opinion was fortified by the highly imaginative conclusions as follows:

HAW [old Saxon] in the North of England means "a green plat in a valley," and it is also used to mean "a small field" or garden connected with the house, as they say *pea-haw*, meaning *pea-field*. It is also the fruit or berry of the *haw*-thorn.

LEY is a field which is laid down to *grass* or *sward*; it is also *a song*. (See Ree's and the London Encyclo-pædias.)

This looked to my fancy like the name of a man who was happy enough to be *singing* while at work in the *field*, and that so habitually as to warrant his neighbors in calling him *Field-singer* or *Fieldsong*.

I thought this all very pretty and quite the thing, until I found later that if the first man of our family got his name in this fashion in Saxondom, he must have emigrated early to Normandy. In Thierry's "Norman Conquest" are to be found as appendices two or three versions of the "Roll of Battle Abbey." No. xii (vol. i., page 417), "Ancient List of the Conquerors of England, published by André Duchesne from a Charter in Battle Abbey," contains among others the names HANSARD, HAST-INGS, HAULAY, etc.

Also in "Another list from Leland," which is in the form of rude couplets, appear

"HASTINGS et HAULLEY, MENEVILLE et MAULEY," etc.

Hence, while mistrusting somewhat my Saxon devices, it may well be imagined with what chagrin I saw myself a Norman; especially when I quote Thierry's language describing the most wretched lot of filibusters that ever left their own or attacked a neighboring country. He says, possibly with some French prejudice (vol. i. p. 161):

"One subscribed for ships, another for armed soldiers, others promised to march in person; priests gave money, merchants merchandize, peasants their goods.

"Presently, after this, the consecrated banner and the bull, authorizing the invasion of England, arrived from Rome, which greatly increased the popular ardour; every one bought what he could; mothers sent their sons to enrol their names for the salvation of their souls. William published his ban in the neighbouring countries; he offered good pay and the pillage of England to every able man who would serve him with lance, sword or cross-bow. A multitude accepted the invitation, coming by every road, far and near, from north and south. They came from Maine and Anjou, from Poitou and Brittany, from France and Flanders, Aquitaine and Burgundy, from the Alps and the banks of the Rhine. All the professional adventurers, all the military vagabonds of Western Europe hastened to Normandy, by long marches; some were knights and chiefs of war, the others simple foot-soldiers and sargeants of arms, as they were then called; some demanded money-pay, others only their passage and all the booty they might make. Some asked for land in England, a domain, a castle, a town; others simply required some rich Saxon in marriage. Every thought, every desire of human avarice presented itself. William rejected *no one*, says the Norman chronicle, and satisfied every one as well as he could."

At page 197 of the same volume, we find the following:

"Another catalogue of the conquerors of England, long-preserved in the treasury of Battle Abby, contained names

"WHAT'S IN A NAME?"

Bouvilain and Boputevilain, Trousselot and Troussebout, L'Engayne and Longue Epee, Œil-de-bœuf and Front-de-bœuf...

Lastly, several authentic documents designate as Norman Knights in England, a *Guillaume le charretier*, a *Hugues le tailleur*, a *Guillaume le tambour*, and among the surnames of the chivalry collected from every corner of Gaul figure a great many mere names of towns and districts-- Saint-Quentin, Saint-Maur, Saint-Denis, Saint-Malo, Tournai, Verdun, Fismes, Chalons, Chaunes, Etampes, Rochefort, La Rochelle, Cahors, Champagne, Gascogne . . .

"Such were the men who assumed in England the titles of *nobleman* and *gentleman*, and planted it there by force of arms themselves and their descendants.

"The mere valet of the Norman man-at-arms, his groom, his lancebearer, became gentleman on the soil of England; they were all at once nobles by the side of the Saxon, once rich and noble himself, but now bending beneath the sword of the foreigner, driven from the home of his ancestors, having nowhere to lay his head."

This, then, seems to be the desperate and detestable crowd of the Eleventh Century (1066) in which the name first appears. Doubtless this disreputable crew furnished the ancestors of many a man who, in later times and under higher culture and finer influences, has become truly noble; but any one will be slow, after reading the foregoing descriptions, in attempting to extract from such a source food for aristocratic pride.

But then again came a letter from my esteemed correspondent, Mr. Christopher E. Hawley of Binghamton, N.Y., containing among other interesting matter the following paragraph which shows that his mind has been running in the direction of the origin of our name:

"1875, Newbrook--'Our English Surnames'--says: 'John Hawley is named in Calendar of Proceedings in Chancery

[Elizabeth]. . . *Hay* or *hawe*--a hedge; hence, de la Haye, de la Hagh. Of simple root comes Hay, Hayes, Haynes, Hawes; composite forms very numerous: Roundhay, Lyndshay, Haywood, Heywood, [Hayward,] Hayland, Hayley. From "*'Haw*, we have Hawley, Haworth, Hawton, Haughton, and probably Featherstonhaugh. We still talk of the Hawthorn and Haw-haw--Chaucer uses the term for a farm-yard or garth-- Chirchay or Chirchehay. Chaucer speaks of the church-hawe as churchyard.' There are other variations, and I believe there is a village in Co. Kent, England, called 'Hageleigh', which is recognized as a variation of *Hawley*."

This, again, looks toward a Saxon origin; but I am quite satisfied that if the names were originally Saxon, its proprietor or his ancestor left his country (possibly "for his country's good"), and having before emigrated to the continent, in due time joined the motley army of the Conqueror, and came again across the channel in the capacity of an invader and Norman.[1]

[1]HR; pvii.

EXPLANATIONS

Individuals are assigned a serial number in the order in which they appear.

The serial number of the parents of a descendant's spouse is the same as the spouse. When looking for a spouse or spouse parents, look for the descendants number first.

Symbols enclosing names
[Brackets] indicate alternate names such as nicknames and alternate spellings.
(P a r e n t h e s e s) indicate maiden names.
{Braces} indicate birth surnames before adoption.

Reference number assignments
Descendant
1. NAME
2. BIRTH
3. BAPTISM
4. DEATH
5. BURIAL
Spouse
6. NAME
7. MARRIAGE
8. BIRTH
9. BAPTISM
10. DEATH
11. BURIAL
12. and up NOTES

ABBREVIATIONS

Capt.	Captain, ships or military
Cem.	cemetery
Co.	county
Col.	Colonel
D.D.	Doctor of Divinity
Dea.	deacon
Gen.	General
ipo	in possession of
Jr.	junior
LL.D.	Doctor of Law
Lt.	Lieutenant
Maj.	Major
M.D.	Physician
n.p.	no place of publication
n.d.	no date of publication.
n.pub.	no publication name
Pvt.	Private
Rev.	Reverend
Sgt.	Sergeant
S.Sgt.	Staff Sergeant
Twp.	township
*	Before child's name, more about this child in the next generation
+	There is an alternate year that is not shown. Example: 1650/1651.

Letters following b. & d. after child's name.
a = after b = before
c = circa (about)

REFERENCE ABBREVIATIONS

CAG   Frederick A. Virkus, Ed.; THE COMPENDIUM OF AMERICAN GENEALOGY; Vol. I, 1925; II, 1926; III, 1928; IV, 1930; V, 1933; VI, 1937; VII, 1942; (Baltimore, MD: The Genealogical Pub., Co., 1987 reprint). (BK88-94)

FC   J. Smith Furthy and Gilbert Cope; THE HISTORY OF CHESTER COUNTY, PENNSYLVANIA; (Philadelphia, PA: Chester Co. Historical Society, Lewis H. Everts, 1881). (BK38)

HR   Elias S. Hawley; THE HAWLEY RECORD; (Buffalo, NY: E. H. Hutchinson & Co., 1890).

IGI   INTERNATIONAL GENEALOGICAL INDEX; (Salt Lake City, UT: Reprinted by permission. Copyright © 1980, 1993 by The Church of the Latter-day Saints).

SHF   The Society of The Hawley Family, Inc.

STATE AND PROVINCE ABBREVIATIONS

United States

Alabama	AL	Montana	MT
Alaska	AK	Nebraska	NE
Arizona	AZ	Nevada	NV
Arkansas	AR	New Hampshire	NH
California	CA	New Jersey	NJ
Canal Zone	CZ	New Mexico	NM
Colorado	CO	New York	NY
Connecticut	CT	North Carolina	NC
Delaware	DE	North Dakota	ND
District of Columbia	DC	Ohio	OH
Florida	FL	Oklahoma	OK
Georgia	GA	Oregon	OR
Guam	GU	Pennsylvania	PA
Hawaii	HI	Puerto Rico	PR
Idaho	ID	Rhode Island	RI
Illinois	IL	South Carolina	SC
Indiana	IN	South Dakota	SD
Iowa	IA	Tennessee	TN
Kansas	KS	Texas	TX
Kentucky	KY	Utah	UT
Louisiana	LA	Vermont	VT
Maine	ME	Virginia	VA
Maryland	MD	Virgin Islands	VI
Massachusetts	MA	Washington	WA
Michigan	MI	West Virginia	WV
Minnesota	MN	Wisconsin	WI
Mississippi	MS	Wyoming	WY
Missouri	MO		

Canada

Alberta	AB	Northwest Territories	NT
British Columbia	BC	Ontario	ON
Manitoba	MB	Prince Edward Island	PE
New Brunswick	NB	Quebec	QC
Newfoundland	NF	Saskatchewan	SK
Nova Scotia	NS	Yukon	YN

FIRST GENERATION

(1) Thomas Hawley, son of _____ and _____ (_____)
Hawley, was born 1654/1655 and married June 26, 1684 in St. Giles
Cripplegate, London, Londonshire, England, **(2) Francis [Maling]
Malin**, daughter of _____ and _____ (_____) [Maling]
Malin, who was born 1662/1663. Thomas died January 1717 and
was buried in Olive, Old Jewry, London, Londonshire, England.
Francis [Maling] died September 10, 1714 and was buried in Olive,
Old Jewry, London, Londonshire, England.

He was a Gunmaker of the Parish of Olive, Old Jewry, London,
England. She was of Paulus Pery [alias Potters Perry],
Northamptonshire, England.

Death date is old style.[12]

References:
1-2, 4, 6, 8, 10, 12. HR; pp420c & 575d.
1, 6. FC; p593. (RGH BK38)
1, 6-7. IGI.

Children:
      3*Thomas Hawley
      4*Anna Hawley
      5*Thomas "again" Hawley
      6*Mary Hawley
      7*Francis Hawley
      8*Susanna Hawley
      9*Sarah Hawley
     10*Joseph Hawley
     11*Thomas "2nd again" Hawley
     12*Benjamin Hawley   b. 5 Oct 1703 d. 29 Jul 1782

SECOND GENERATION

(3) Thomas Hawley, son of Thomas and Francis [Maling] (Malin) Hawley, died young.[12]

References:
1, 12. HR; p575d.

(4) Anna Hawley, daughter of Thomas and Francis [Maling] (Malin) Hawley.

References:
1. HR; p575d.

(5) Thomas "again" Hawley, son of Thomas and Francis [Maling] (Malin) Hawley, died young.[12]

References:
1, 12. HR; p575d.

(6) Mary Hawley, daughter of Thomas and Francis [Maling] (Malin) Hawley.

References:
1. HR; p575d.

(7) Francis Hawley, son of Thomas and Francis [Maling] (Malin) Hawley.
References:
1. HR; p575d.

(8) Susanna Hawley, daughter of Thomas and Francis [Maling] (Malin) Hawley.

References:
1. HR; p575d.

(9) Sarah Hawley, daughter of Thomas and Francis [Maling] (Malin) Hawley.

References:
1. HR; p575d.

(10) Joseph Hawley, son of Thomas and Francis [Maling] (Malin) Hawley.

References:
1. HR; p575d.

(11) Thomas "2nd again" Hawley, son of Thomas and Francis [Maling] (Malin) Hawley.

References:
1. HR; p575d.

(12) Benjamin Hawley, son of Thomas and Francis [Maling] (Malin) Hawley, was born October 5, 1703 in London, Londonshire, England, and married January 5, 1730 in Parish of Giles, in the Fields, Londonshire, London, England, **(13) Dinah Gabiter**, daughter of John and _____ (_____) Gabiter, who was born November 6, 1698 in Parish of Giles, in the Fields, London, England. Benjamin died July 29, 1782 and was buried July 30, 1782 in Friends Cemetery, Birmingham, Huntingdon County, Pennsylvania. Dinah died November 26, 1761 in Birmingham Township, Chester County, Pennsylvania and was buried in Birmingham Township, Chester County, Pennsylvania.

He was a Quaker of Birmingham Township, Chester County, Pennsylvania. She was a Quaker of the Parish of Giles in the Fields, Londonshire, England. Dates are old style.[12]

Being a member of the Religious Society of Friends (Quakers), Benjamin was opposed to the treatment given Quakers in England at that time, so he at the age of 18 immigrated to America and landed in Pennsylvania in the spring of 1722. He settled in the Township of Thornsbury,

Chester County, Pennsylvania where he took up residence with a friend of the family, John Willes. He started teaching in that area.

During the late winter of 1729, Benjamin returned to England and on January 5, 1730, he married Dinah Gabiter, daughter of John of the Parish of Giles in the Fields, London. She was born November 6, 1698 in the Parish of Giles.

They set sail for America and settled in Birmingham Township, Chester County, Pennsylvania on the forks of the Brandywine River, where he followed farming and teaching school. Birmingham Township was organized in 1686.

A Bible printed in 1599, was given him by his sister Mary in 1735-36, and it contained the birth dates of his children.

In 1735 Benjamin took a voyage to England and returned the following spring making also other voyages in 1759 and 1769 on family estate matters.

The date of erection of the western end of the Birmingham Meeting Hall has been fixed at 1765, but Benjamin notes in his diary June 13, 1763, that in the afternoon he "went to the raising of ye meeting house", at this time he was teaching school nearby.

A James Dilworth was said to have built the first house, a log hut where Dilworth Town now stands and the Tavern Building in 1758, though there was no tavern kept there until after his death, when his son Charles obtained a license. Charles was a prominent citizen and frequently concerned in public affairs, however, he was disowned by the Friend's Society for taking an active part in Revolutionary matters. Benjamin notes in his diary August 27, 1770, that he "went to the raising of Charles Dilworth's sign"--no doubt this was made the occasion for much drinking and hilarity.

The battle of Brandywine, as is known to most of our people, was fought on two different fields--at Birmingham and at Chad's Ford. The British Army, soon after leaving Kennet Square on the march eastward, formed into two divisions.

One of them, under command of General Knyphausen, marched directly to Chad's Ford in Delaware County and the other, under the command of General Cornwallis and

General Cornwallis and accompanied by General Howe, the Commander-in-Chief, taking a northerly direction, crossing the West Branch of the Brandywine at Trimble's Ford and the East Branch at Jeffer's Ford, then turning southward to Birmingham.

In the fight at Birmingham Meeting House, a party of Americans for a time, occupied a position inside the rear wall of the graveyard. A number of British fell here. The killed of both Armies who fell in the vicinity of the meeting house were buried in the graveyard which partly surrounds it, their remains occupying one common grave just inside the gate and on the side next to the meeting house. The British used the meeting house as a hospital while they remained in the neighborhood.

When General Washington resolved to dispute the passage of the Brandywine by the British Army, and for that purpose marched his forces to it's banks, he took possession of the Birmingham Meeting House intending to use it as a hospital for the sick of his army.

During much of this time, Benjamin was farming a place belonging to his son William

near Concord. He writes in his diary:

"9/29/77. Yesterday the sick soldiers took possession of ye meeting house" [probably Concord]. And on the 31st [1st day], he notes that his son John and Jane (Jeffers) "Went to meeting at Newlin".
9/9/77 "The soldiers came by for fowl and milk."
9/11/77 "Fifth day very hot, finished harrowing the rye, son William came and took his horse, the English engaged the Americans, latter defeated with much loss." 9/12/77 "Sixth day cloudy, putting up fences Americans made down in their retreat."
9/13/77 "Seventh day, some clouds, some of ye English soldiers had sundries to ye value of 8s (shillings) and didn't pay."
9/14/77 "First day at home, Jane 49 weeks, the soldiers came and had milk, bread and pye."
9/15/77 "Second day do rcd of ye soldiers about 10s, lost an ax, 2 bags and iron pote, threshed 3dz."
9/16/77 "Third day cloudy, English soldiers went away, thrashed 2dz, Rachel Miller and Isaac came to visit. This PM very hard rain."

He arrived from his last trip to England on September 19, 1769 and taking sometime to settle his affairs he undertook school keeping again in December following and continued till August 1770. His hearing failing which rendered him incapable of that employment. The 3rd of April he moved to the Taylor's and worked her place on the shares for one year. Then moved to live on a place of his son (William) in Concord and followed farming, but finding a failure of nature and unable to manage his business he grew uneasy with his way of living and expressed a desire of living with some of his children. Accordingly he moved the 13th April 1778 to his son Joseph in West Bradford to live in a part of his house and continued with his wife upwards of 4 years, till after a lingering disorder of a kind of dropsy and difficulty of breathing, which the afflicting he bore with a good degree of patience and resignation for upwards of one year with some small intermission.

He departed this life the 29th of July 1782 about two o'clock in the morning and was buried in Friends burying ground at Birmingham the day following, beside his first wife Dinah, aged 78 years and nearly ten months.

His Bible is now in the possession of Rebecca (Hawley) Chambers. His gun barrel which he brought from England, is in the possession of his great grandson, Thomas P. Hawley of West Chester, Pennsylvania, who has refitted it.[13]

One of my relatives has a short account of my great great grandfather, Benjamin Hawley, written about himself, of which I quote a part, as follows:

"My father's name was Thomas Hawley, citizen and gunmaker, London, in the parish of Olive, Old Jewry, at the corner next Coleman Street and Lothbury. My mother was Frances Malin of a village called Paulus Pery [alias Potters Perry], Northamptonshire, by whom he had (10) children, five sons and five daughters, whose names being worked on a sampler were:

> Thomas and Anna, Thomas and Mary,
> Frances, Susanna and Sarah,
> Joseph and Thomas and little Benjamin;
> Thomas and Frances had these children ten.

I was born on the 5th day of the 8th month, called October, in the year of our Lord, 1703, old style.

My mother departed this life on the 10th day of the 7th month, called September, in the year of our Lord, 1714, old style, in the 52nd year of her age, and was buried in the grave-yard belonging to the Parish Church of Olive, Old Jewry. My father lived in widowhood until sometime in the month, aforsaid, in the 63rd year of his age, and was buried in the same grave with my mother.

My sister put me out apprentice to John Horsey, gunmaker, London, with whom I staid until the month called July 1722, when I left him and went on board the BRITANNICA, John Head, master, bound for Maderia and Philadelphia, [a short history of the voyage is given].

I was married to my first wife Dinah Gabiter, of the Parish of Giles in the fields, London, by her I had four sons and two daughters. My wife died 26th of 11th month, 1761."[14]

Benjamin was on the 1753 tax rolls and was listed as a land owner in 1774, East Bradford, Pennsylvania.[13]

References:

1-2, 4, 10, 12. HR; pp420c, 575d & 576a. Originally from BENJAMIN HAWLEY-HIS BOOK; (Sewell's History. Bought of Luke Kind in George Yard, Lombard Street, London, 1759).

1-2, 4, 6-8, 10, 13. FC; pp73, 234, 524 & 593. (RGH BK38)

14. Portions of a letter dated April 26, 1887 from Richard Moore of Philadelphia, Pennsylvania to Elias S. Hawley and printed in the Hawley Record, Page 575.

Children:

14*Benjamin Hawley, Jr.	b. 18 Nov 1730	d. 26 Oct 1815
15*Mary Hawley	b. 5 Oct 1732	
16*Joseph Hawley	b. 21 Mar 1735	d. 21 Nov 1817
17*William Hawley	b. 17 Sep 1737	d. 2 Jun 1826
18*Susannah [Susan] Hawley	b. 28 Mar 1740	d. 21 Jul 1770
19*John Hawley	b. 11 Mar 1743+	

He also married April 20, 1763 in Birmingham Township, Chester County, Pennsylvania, **(20) Catharine [Hebourne] Hillborn**, daughter of _____ and _____ (_____) Hillborn, who was born February 1696. Catharine [Hebourne] died May 13, 1789.

Her name may have been Hebourne as recorded in the Hawley Record. Married at Birmingham Meeting, Chester County, Pennsylvania. After Benjamin's death she removed, in about a month, to live with her relations [it being her choice] and continued very feeble and infirm for nearly 7 years. She departed this life the 13th of the 5th month 1789, aged 93 years and 3 months. She was of Birmingham, Pennsylvania.[12]

References:

1, 6-8, 10, 12. HR; p575d.
1, 6-7. FC; p593. (RGH BK38)

THIRD GENERATION

(14) Benjamin Hawley, Jr., son of Benjamin and Dinah (Gabiter) Hawley, was born November 18, 1730 in Birmingham Township, Chester County, Pennsylvania, and married April 22, 1756 in E. Bradford Township, Chester County, Pennsylvania, **(21) Mary Johnson**, daughter of Benjamin Robert and Katherine (Knott) Johnson, who was born May 18, 1733 in East Bradford Township, Chester County, Pennsylvania. Benjamin, Jr., died October 26, 1815 in West Bradford Township, Chester Co., Pennsylvania. Mary died April 7, 1822 in East Bradford Township, Chester County, Pennsylvania.

He was a Teacher and Farmer.[12] She was of East Bradford, Chester County, Pennsylvania and they settled there. He served as a Private in the Pennsylvania Militia.[13]

References:
1-2, 6, 8, 12. HR; pp420c & 575d.
1-2, 4, 6-7, 13. FC; p593. (RGH BK38)

Children:

22*Caleb Hawley	b. 23 Apr 1757	d.	1822
23*Thomas Hawley	b. 6 Feb 1758	d. 17 Apr 1781	
24*Joseph Hawley	b. 6 Jun 1760	d. 5 Oct 1856	
25*Robert Hawley	b. 28 Mar 1762	d. 16 Jul 1829	
26*Rachel Hawley	b. 3 Aug 1763		
27*Hannah Hawley	b. 7 Apr 1766		
28*Mary Hawley	b. 2 Sep 1767		
29*Lydia Hawley	b. 28 Feb 1769	d. 28 Dec 1770	
30*Susanna Hawley	b. 11 Sep 1770		
31*Tamer Hawley	b. 2 May 1772		
32*Rebecca Hawley	b. 9 Jan 1774	d. 18 Mar 1859	
33*Dinah Hawley	b. 18 Jan 1777		
34*Benjamin Hawley	b. 18 May 1777	d. 17 Aug 1857	
35*Phebe Hawley	b. 14 Jan 1779	d. 11 Feb 1782	

(15) Mary Hawley, daughter of Benjamin and Dinah (Gabiter) Hawley, was born October 5, 1732 in Birmingham Township, Chester County, Pennsylvania, and married **(36) Hugh Kirgan**.

She was of Chester County, Pennsylvania.[12]

References:
1-2, 12. HR; p420a.
1-2, 6. FC; p593. (RGH BK38)

(16) Joseph Hawley, son of Benjamin and Dinah (Gabiter) Hawley, was born March 21, 1735 in Birmingham Township, Chester County, Pennsylvania, and married March 28, 1762 in Malemsbury, Wiltshire, England, **(37) Elizabeth Spackman**, daughter of Issac and Esther (_____) Spackman, who was born September 21, 1735 in Malemsbury, Wiltshire, England. Joseph died November 21, 1817 in West Bradford Township, Chester County, Pennsylvania and was buried in West Bradford Township, Chester County, Pennsylvania. Elizabeth died August 25, 1796.

He was a Farmer of Birmingham and West Bradford, Pennsylvania. She was of Malemsbury, Wiltshire, England and West Bradford. They were Quakers and were married in Bradford Meeting House.

Joseph subscribed, with others, to provide money for building a bridge across the east branch of Brandywine Creek East Bradford at Taylor's Ford. He was a land owner 1774 East and West Bradford.[12]

References:
1-2. HR; p420c.
1-2, 4, 6-8, 10, 12. FC; pp165-167, 593, 729. (RGH BK38)

Children:

38*Esther Hawley	b. 18 Feb 1763	d. 28 Oct 1816	
39*Dinah Hawley	b. 21 Dec 1764	d. 24 Dec 1768	
40*William Hawley	b. 18 Jul 1766	d. 8 May 1836	
41*Mary Hawley	b. 14 Sep 1768	d. 15 Sep 1771	
42*Elizabeth Hawley	b. 29 May 1770	d. 22 Sep 1852	
43*Joseph Hawley, Jr.	b. 12 Nov 1771	d. 21 Dec 1851	
44*Issac Hawley	b. 6 Aug 1775	d.	1837
45*John Hawley	b. 25 Sep 1778	d.c	1814

He also married April 3, 1800 in West Bradford Township, Chester County, Pennsylvania, **(46) Agnes Davis**, daughter of Evan and Susanna (Jones) Davis, who was born December 1, 1745/1746. Agnes died August 2, 1818.

She was a Quaker of Birmingham and West Bradford, Pennsylvania. They were married in Bradford Meeting House, being her third husband. She was previously married to _____ Davis.[12]

References:
1, 6-8, 10, 12. FC; p593. (RGH BK38)

(17) William Hawley, son of Benjamin and Dinah (Gabiter) Hawley, was born September 17, 1737 in Birmingham Township, Chester County, Pennsylvania, and married November 15, 1764 in Concord, Chester County, Pennsylvania, **(47) Hannah Taylor**, daughter of _____ and _____ (_____) Taylor. William died June 2, 1826 in Birmingham Township, Chester County, Pennsylvania.

References:
1-2. HR; p420c.
1, 6-7. IGI.
1-2, 4, 6. FC; p593. (RGH BK38)

He also married April 26, 1840, **(48) Hannah Frame**, daughter of _____ and _____ (_____) Frame.

References:
1, 6. FC; p593. (RGH BK38)
1, 6-7. IGI.

He also married **(49) Elizabeth Eavenson**, daughter of _____ and _____ (_____) Eavenson.

References:
1, 6. FC; p593. (RGH BK38)

He also married **(50) Phebe Hoopes**, daughter of _____ and _____ (_____) Hoopes.

References:
1, 6. FC; p593. (RGH BK38)

(18) **Susannah [Susan] Hawley**, daughter of Benjamin and Dinah (Gabiter) Hawley, was born March 28, 1740 in Birmingham Township, Chester County, Pennsylvania, and married (51) **Christopher Nupher**, son of _____ and _____ (_____) Nupher. Susannah [Susan] died July 21, 1770. They were of Chester County, Pennsylvania.[12]

References:
1-2, 6, 12. HR; p420c.
1-2, 4, 6. FC; p593. (BK38)

(19) **John Hawley**, son of Benjamin and Dinah (Gabiter) Hawley, was born March 11, 1743/1745 in Birmingham Township, Chester County, Pennsylvania.

References:
1-2. HR; p420c.
1-2. FC; p593. (RGH BK38)

FOURTH GENERATION

(22) Caleb Hawley, son of Benjamin, Jr., and Mary (Johnson) Hawley, was born April 23, 1757 in East Bradford Township, Chester County, Pennsylvania, and married May 30, 1782 in E. Bradford Township, Chester County, Pennsylvania, **(52) Hannah Batten**, daughter of _____ and _____ (_____) Batten, who was born March 1759 in East Bradford Township, Chester County, Pennsylvania. Caleb died 1822 in Middleton Township, Columbiana County, Ohio and was buried in Ohio.

He was of Chester County, Pennsylvania. They lived in Columbiana County, Ohio.[12]

On June 27, 1801, Caleb and wife Hannah and children: Nathan, David, Amos, Caleb, Benjamin, Mary, Richard, Jesse, Elisha and Hannah Rocf Bradford Monthly Meeting, dated May 15, 1801.

On April 21, 1823, Hannah, Sr. and Hannah, Jr. Gct Salem Monthly Meeting.

On April 23, 1823, Hannah, Sr. and Hannah, Jr. Rocf Middleton Monthly Meeting dated April 21, 1823.

On May 22, 1828 Hannah recrg (H).

On July 24, 1828 Hannah Gct Salem Monthly Meeting.[13]

References:
1, 6, 8, 13. MONTHLY MEETING NOTES; Westland, IN; pp631, 718 & 821. (RGH MI1)
1-2, 6, 12. HR; pp420d, 520c & 576a.
1-2, 4, 6-7. FC; p593 & xxiii. (RGH BK38)

Children:

53*David Hawley	b. 30 Oct 1782	
54*Nathan Hawley	b. 17 Feb 1784	
55*Amos Hawley	b. 5 Mar 1786	
56*Caleb Hawley, Jr.	b. 28 May 1788	d. 19 Jul 1878
57*Benjamin Hawley	b. 20 Jul 1790	d. 27 Feb 1875
58*Mary Hawley	b. 19 Jun 1792	
59*Richard Hawley	b. 1 Mar 1794	
60*Jessie Hawley	b. 11 Feb 1796	d. 31 Jul 1880
61*Elisha Hawley	b. 21 Nov 1798	d. 14 Jun 1884
62*Thomas Hawley	b. 1802	
63*Hannah Hawley	b. 1804	d. 8 May 1880

(23) **Thomas Hawley**, son of Benjamin, Jr., and Mary (Johnson) Hawley, was born February 6, 1758 in East Bradford Township, Chester County, Pennsylvania. Thomas died April 17, 1781 in East Bradford Township, Chester County, Pennsylvania and was buried April 19, 1781 in Bradford Township, Chester County, Pennsylvania.

References:
1-2. HR; p576a.
1-2, 4-5. FC; p593. (RGH BK38)

(24) **Joseph Hawley**, son of Benjamin, Jr., and Mary (Johnson) Hawley, was born June 6, 1760 in Bradford Township, Chester County, Pennsylvania, and married May 23, 1793, (64) **Rebecca Meredith**, daughter of Simon and Dinah (Pugh) Meredith, who was born October 8, 1766. Joseph died October 5, 1856 in Uwchlan, Chester County, Pennsylvania. Rebecca died June 12, 1851. They were of Uwchlan, Pennsylvania.[12]

References:
1-2, 4, 6-8, 10. HR; pp420c-421a & 575a.
1-2, 4, 6-8, 12. FC; pp593, 656. (RGH BK38)

Children:

65*Mary Hawley	b.	1799	d.	1822
66*Simon Hawley	b.	1801	d.	1863
67*Benjamin Hawley	b.	1803	d.	1850
68*Joel Hawley	b.	7 Oct 1804		
69*Jesse Hawley	b.	5 Feb 1806	d.	1887
70*Dinah Hawley			d.b	1890

(25) **Robert Hawley**, son of Benjamin, Jr., and Mary (Johnson) Hawley, was born March 28, 1762 in East Bradford Township, Chester County, Pennsylvania, and married November 21, 1787 in Concord, Delaware County, Pennsylvania, (71) **Patience Yearsley**, daughter of Thomas and _____ (_____) Yearsley, who was born in Chester County, Pennsylvania. Robert died July 16, 1829 in Muncy, Lycoming County, Pennsylvania. Patience died December 5, 1828 in Muncy, Lycoming County, Pennsylvania.

He was of Muncy, Pennsylvania in 1802. She was of Chester County, Pennsylvania.[12]

References:
1-2, 4, 6, 10. HR; pp420c, 421b & 575a.
1-2, 6-7, 12. FC; p593. (RGH BK38)

Children:
    72*Gideon Hawley
    73*Mary Hawley
    74*Robert Hawley
    75*Enos Hawley   b. 10 Jun 1799
    76*Mary "again" Hawley
    77*Hannah Hawley

(26) Rachel Hawley, daughter of Benjamin, Jr., and Mary (Johnson) Hawley, was born August 3, 1763 in East Bradford Township, Chester County, Pennsylvania, and married **(78) Arthur McCann**, son of _____ and _____ (_____) McCann.

References:
1-2. HR; pp420c & 576a.
1-2, 6. FC; p593. (RGH BK38)

(27) Hannah Hawley, daughter of Benjamin, Jr., and Mary (Johnson) Hawley, was born April 7, 1766 in East Bradford Township, Chester County, Pennsylvania.

References:
1-2. HR; p576a.
1-2. FC; p593. (RGH BK38)

(28) Mary Hawley, daughter of Benjamin, Jr., and Mary (Johnson) Hawley, was born September 2, 1767 in East Bradford Township, Chester County, Pennsylvania, and married **(79) John Ingram**, son of _____ and _____ (_____) Ingram.

References:
1-2. HR; p576a.
1-2, 6. FC; p593. (RGH BK38)

(29) Lydia Hawley, daughter of Benjamin, Jr., and Mary (Johnson) Hawley, was born February 28, 1769 in East Bradford Township, Chester County, Pennsylvania. Lydia died December 28, 1770 in East Bradford Township, Chester County, Pennsylvania and was buried December 29, 1770 in Bradford Township, Chester County, Pennsylvania.
She was of East Bradford Township, Pennsylvania.[12]

References:
1-2, 12. HR; p576a.
1-2, 4-5. FC; p593. (RGH BK38)

(30) Susanna Hawley, daughter of Benjamin, Jr., and Mary (Johnson) Hawley, was born September 11, 1770 and married December 12, 1793 in West Bradford Township, Chester County, Pennsylvania, **(80) Elisha Davis**, son of _____ and _____ (_____) Davis.

References:
1-2. HR; p576a.
1-2, 6-7. FC; p593. (RGH BK38)

(31) Tamer Hawley, daughter of Benjamin, Jr., and Mary (Johnson) Hawley, was born May 2, 1772 in East Bradford Township, Chester County, Pennsylvania, and married December 17, 1801 in East Bradford Township, Chester County, Pennsylvania, **(81) Joshua Hicklin**, son of _____ and _____ (_____) Hicklin.
Has marriage in Wilmington, Delaware.[12]

References:
1-2, 6-7. FC; p593. (RGH BK38)
1, 6-7, 12. IGI.

Children:
    82*Hannah Hicklin
    83*Jesse Hicklin

(32) Rebecca Hawley, daughter of Benjamin, Jr., and Mary (Johnson) Hawley, was born January 9, 1774 in East Bradford Township, Chester County, Pennsylvania. Rebecca died March 18,

1859 in Chester County, Pennsylvania and was buried March 30, 1859 in Goshen Township, Chester County, Pennsylvania. She was not married. She was of Goshen Township, Pennsylvania and died at Aaron Garret's house. There were three Aarons, the first born December 27, 1746, died March 18, 1815, son of Samuel, Jr. of Willistown, Pennsylvania; his son Aaron, Jr. married Jane Hoopes; his son Aaron married _____ _____. Anyway, it was in Chester County, Pennsylvania.[12]

References:
1-2. HR; p576a.
1-2, 4-5, 12. FC; pp561, 593. (RGH BK38)

(33) Dinah Hawley, daughter of Benjamin, Jr., and Mary (Johnson) Hawley, was born January 18, 1777 in East Bradford Township, Chester County, Pennsylvania, and married May 21, 1801 in E. Bradford Township, Chester County, Pennsylvania, **(84) John Hicklin**, son of _____ and _____ (_____) Hicklin.

References:
1-2. HR; p576a.
1-2, 6-7. FC; p593. (RGH BK38)

(34) Benjamin Hawley, son of Benjamin, Jr., and Mary (Johnson) Hawley, was born May 18, 1777 in East Bradford Township, Chester County, Pennsylvania, and married March 26, 1801 in E. Bradford Township, Chester County, Pennsylvania, **(85) Deborah Hoopes**, daughter of _____ and _____ (_____) Hoopes. Benjamin died August 17, 1857 in East Bradford Township, Chester County, Pennsylvania.
They had a large family.[12]

References:
1-2, 12. HR; p576a.
1-2, 4, 6-7. FC; p593. (RGH BK38)

Children:
    86*Mary Hawley   b. 11 Jul 1803

(35) **Phebe Hawley**, daughter of Benjamin, Jr., and Mary (Johnson) Hawley, was born January 14, 1779 in East Bradford Township, Chester County, Pennsylvania. Phebe died February 11, 1782 in East Bradford Township, Chester County, Pennsylvania and was buried February 13, 1782 in Bradford Township, Chester County, Pennsylvania.

References:
1. HR; p576a.
1-2, 4-5. FC; p593. (RGH BK38)

(38) **Esther Hawley**, daughter of Joseph and Elizabeth (Spackman) Hawley, was born February 18, 1763 in West Bradford Township, Chester County, Pennsylvania, and married April 28, 1791 in Bradford Township, Chester County, Pennsylvania, (87) **Daniel Kent**, son of William and Anna (_____) Kent, who was born 1765. Esther died October 28, 1816. Daniel died 1844.

They were Quakers of Goshen, Pennsylvania. Daniel came from Limerick, Ireland to Philadelphia, Pennsylvania in 1785 at the age of 20.

Daniel was a cutler by trade and in the twentieth year of his age, as business was dull and he could not get constant employment, he determined to try his fortune in America. While searching for work in Waterford, and failing to obtain any, he found a vessel, the brigantine "Asia," about to set sail for Philadelphia. He availed himself of this opportunity to come to this country, and bound himself by indenture to John Johnson, master, in the sum of ten pounds ten shillings, British sterling money, as payment for passage, and what ever more money that might appear by receipts to be advanced for necessaries. This indenture was entered into May 21, 1785. He arrived in Philadelphia July 26th, being nine weeks and two days on the passage. On August 27th the said John Johnson, for the consideration of fourteen pounds and ten shillings, in hand paid, signed over the indenture to Joseph Hawley, he fulfilling the part therein mentioned. And on the same papers a certificate of Joseph Hawley, stating that the said Daniel Kent fulfilled the indenture honestly, and that his conduct and conversation has been orderly so far as came to his knowledge. Signed by his hand the 26th day of 8th month, 1788. In 1786, the next year after he arrived in this country, a certificate was sent to him signed by about thirty persons, stated to be men of consequence, certifying to his pious education and good conduct, and that he departed from his father without cause or compulsion, in a state of innocence, without vice or blemish, and they certify that from their knowledge of him while under his father's care he was worthy of notice.

Although brought up a Methodist, after living with Joseph a few years, who was a member of the Religious Society of Friends, he became a member of the same meeting. In 1790 he was received into the membership of Caln Meeting and the following year he married Joseph's daughter Esther at Bradford Meeting.

He afterwards purchased a farm in East Fallowfield, Pennsylvania where most of their children were born.

In 1795 he was granted a certificate from Bradford to Kennet; from Kennet to Bradford in 1797 and from Bradford to Londongrove, all in Pennsylvania April 13, 1798.

He held office of Justice of the Peace by appointment of the Governor for about twenty years.[12]

References:
1-2, 4. CAG; Vol. 1, p174. (RGH BK87)
1-2, 4, 6-8, 10, 12. FC; pp593, 620-621. (RGH BK38)

Children:

88*William Kent	b. 3 Aug 1792	d. 15 Oct 1860	
89*Joseph Kent	b. 30 Jun 1794	d. 13 Jul 1863	
90*Elizabeth Kent	b. 19 Apr 1796	d. 14 Aug 1848	
91*Ann Kent	b. 22 Jun 1798		
92*Mary Kent	b. 29 Dec 1800		
93*Daniel Kent	b. 22 Feb 1803		
94*Benjamin Kent	b. 23 Mar 1805	d.	1881

(39) Dinah Hawley, daughter of Joseph and Elizabeth (Spackman) Hawley, was born December 21, 1764 in West Bradford Township, Chester County, Pennsylvania. Dinah died December 24, 1768 in West Bradford Township, Chester County, Pennsylvania.
She was a Quaker.[12]

References:
1-2, 4, 12. FC; p593. (RGH BK38)

(40) William Hawley, son of Joseph and Elizabeth (Spackman) Hawley, was born July 18, 1766 and married **(95) Ann Marshall**, daughter of _____ and _____ (_____) Marshall. William died May 8, 1836.
They were Quakers. Had sons in Chester and Lancaster Counties, Pennsylvania.[12]

References:
1, 6, 12. HR; p421c.
1-2, 4, 6, 12. FC; p593. (RGH BK38)

(41) Mary Hawley, daughter of Joseph and Elizabeth (Spackman) Hawley, was born September 14, 1768 in West Bradford Township, Chester County, Pennsylvania. Mary died September 15, 1771.
She was a Quaker.[12]

References:
1-2, 4, 12. FC; p593. (RGH BK38)

(42) Elizabeth Hawley, daughter of Joseph and Elizabeth (Spackman) Hawley, was born May 29, 1770 in West Bradford Township, Chester County, Pennsylvania, and married **(96) Richard Woodward**, son of _____ and _____ (_____) Woodward. Elizabeth died September 22, 1852.

They were Quakers.[12]

References:
1-2, 4, 6, 12. FC; p593. (RGH BK38)

(43) Joseph Hawley, Jr., son of Joseph and Elizabeth (Spackman) Hawley, was born November 12, 1771 in West Bradford Township, Chester County, Pennsylvania, and married **(97) Elizabeth Woodward**, daughter of _____ and _____ (_____) Woodward. Joseph, Jr., died December 21, 1851 in West Bradford Township, Chester County, Pennsylvania.

References:
1. HR; p421c.
1-2, 4, 6. FC; p593. (RGH BK38)

Children:
```
98*_____ Hawley
99*_____ Hawley
```

(44) Issac Hawley, son of Joseph and Elizabeth (Spackman) Hawley, was born August 6, 1775 in West Bradford Township, Chester County, Pennsylvania. Issac died 1837 in Downingstown Township, Chester County, Pennsylvania.

He was a Quaker of Downingtown, Pennsylvania.[13] He was not married.[12]

References:
1, 12. HR; p421c.
1-2, 4, 13. FC; p593. (RGH BK38)

(45) **John Hawley**, son of Joseph and Elizabeth (Spackman) Hawley, was born September 25, 1778 in West Bradford Township, Chester County, Pennsylvania. John died about 1814 in West Bradford Township, Chester County, Pennsylvania.

He was a Quaker. He was not married. His Will was dated May 22, 1814; contents not known.[12]

References:
1-2, 4, 12. FC; p593. (RGH BK38)

FIFTH GENERATION

(53) David Hawley, son of Caleb and Hannah (Batten) Hawley, was born October 30, 1782 in East Bradford Township, Chester County, Pennsylvania, and married August 17, 1809 in Fairfield Township, Columbiana County, Ohio, **(100) Rachel Beal**, daughter of Joseph and Hannah (_____) Beal.

They were Quakers.[12] She says he died at age 16. The dates don't match.[13]

References:
1, 6. HR; p420d.
1-2. PEDIGREE CHART; Edna Risdom Neary; Cedar Rapids, IA; ipo SHF 8 May 1990. (RGH PN2)
1, 6-7, 12. MONTHLY MEETING NOTES; Westland Meeting House, IN; p631. (RGH MI1)
1, 13. Ruama (Coit) Hawley; Tulsa, OK to SHF 2 Aug 1967. (RGH PN1)

(54) Nathan Hawley, son of Caleb and Hannah (Batten) Hawley, was born February 17, 1784 in East Bradford Township, Chester County, Pennsylvania, and married 1808, **(101) Hannah Eveson**, daughter of _____ and _____ (_____) Eveson.

They were Quakers. On February 24, 1802, Nathan was dismissed for disunity.[12]

References:
1, 6. HR; p420d.
1-2, 6-8, 12. MONTHLY MEETING NOTES; Westland Meeting House, IN; pp37 & 718. (RGH MI1)

Children:

102*Edward [Emanuel] D. Hawley	b.	25 Oct 1808
103*Milton Hawley	b.	22 Feb 1810
104*Mellon Hawley	b.	22 Feb 1810
105*Calib Hawley	b.	2 Jan 1812
106*Aaron Hawley	b.	2 Feb 1814
107*Jesse Hawley	b.	1 Aug 1816
108*Mary Hawley	b.	25 Dec 1819
109*Benjamin Hawley	b.	23 Oct 1821

```
110*Cynthia Hawley          b. 12 Oct 1823
111*Jane Hawley             b. 20 Mar 1826
```

(55) Amos Hawley, son of Caleb and Hannah (Batten) Hawley, was born March 5, 1786 in East Bradford Township, Chester County, Pennsylvania, and married **(112) Mary Warrington**, daughter of _____ and _____ (_____) Warrington.

They were Quakers. On December 8, 1810 he was dismissed for disunity.[12]

References:
1. HR; p420d.
1, 12. MONTHLY MEETING NOTES; Westland Meeting House, IN; p631. (RGH MI1)
1-2. PEDIGREE CHART; Edna R. Neary; Cedar Rapids, IA; ipo SHF 8 May 1990. (RGH PN2)

(56) Caleb Hawley, Jr., son of Caleb and Hannah (Batten) Hawley, was born May 28, 1788 in East Bradford Township, Chester County, Pennsylvania, and married October 15, 1817 in Elkrun Township, Columbiana County, Ohio, **(113) Catharine James**, daughter of Issac and Sarah (_____) James. Caleb, Jr., died July 19, 1878 in Gower Township, Cedar County, Iowa and was buried in Honey Grove Cemetery, Gower Township, Cedar County, Iowa. Catharine died 1845 in Marlborough Township, Stark County, Ohio and was buried in Marlborough Township, Stark County, Ohio.

They were Quakers of Gower Township, Cedar County, Iowa.[13]

On May 17, 1819, Caleb and wife Catherine and son Joseph, Gct New Garden Monthly Meeting.

On June 24, 1819, Caleb and wife Catherine and son Joseph Rocf Middleton Monthly Meeting dated May 17, 1819.

On December 20th, Calib, Jr. was among the prominent members of the newly formed Sandy Spring Monthly Meeting in Columbiana County, Ohio. On April 27, 1821, Calib and wife Catherine and children Gct White Water, Indiana Monthly Meeting.

On July 17, 1824, Calib and wife Catherine and children Joseph, Benjamin & Phebe Ann Rocf White Water Monthly Meeting, dated May 15, 1824.

On May 16, 1829, Caleb and wife Catherine and children Joseph, Benjamin, Phebe Ann, James, Latham and Caleb Gct Marlborough Monthly Meeting, Ohio. Marlborough later changed to Deer Creek in 1848.[12]

References:
1. HR; p420d.
1-2. PEDIGREE CHART; Edna R. Neary; Cedar Rapids, IA; ipo SHF 8 May 1990. (RGH PN2)
1, 6-7, 12. MONTHLY MEETING NOTES; Westland, IN; pp631, 821, 871 & 906. (RGH MI1)
1, 4, 6, 10, 13. Robert A. Hawley; West Palm Beach, FL to SHF; Jul 1989. (RGH FG1)

Children:

114*Joseph Hawley	b. 30 Jun 1818	d. 11 Dec 1905
115*Benjamin Hawley	b. 20 May 1820	d. 20 Jun 1894
116*Phebe Ann Hawley	b. 3 Sep 1822	
117*James G. Hawley	b. 10 Dec 1825	d. 3 Sep 1917
118*Latham Hawley	b. 7 Oct 1827	d. 10 Jun 1905
119*Caleb P. Hawley	b. 10 Feb 1829	
120*Sarah Hawley	b. 1 Mar 1833	d. 9 Oct 1895

He also married October 21, 1847 in Carmel Township, Columbiana County, Ohio, **(121) Tacy Hole**, daughter of David and Anna (_____) Hole.

She was a Quaker of Columbiana County, Ohio. On December 18, 1847 Tacy Gct Marlborough Monthly Meeting.[12]

References:
1, 6-7, 12. MONTHLY MEETING NOTES; Westland, IN; p871. (RGH MI1)

(57) Benjamin Hawley, son of Caleb and Hannah (Batten) Hawley, was born July 20, 1790 in East Bradford Township, Chester County, Pennsylvania, and married February 2, 1825 in Salem Township, Columbiana County, Ohio, **(122) Mary Davis**, daughter of Samuel and Mary (_____) Davis, who was born August 10, 1791. Benjamin died February 27, 1875. Mary died July 4, 1869.

They were Quakers. They came from Pennsylvania to Ohio in 1802, voted in 1809.[12]

On May 19, 1823 Benjamin Gct Salem Meeting House.
On May 22, 1828, Benjamin and wife Mary and children Eliza and Sarah recrg.
On July 24, 1828, Benjamin and wife Mary and children Eliza and Sarah Gct Salem Monthly Meeting, Pennsylvania.
On July 30, 1828, Benjamin and wife Mary Rocf New Garden Monthly Meeting, Indiana dated July 24, 1828.
On August 20, 1828, Benjamin discharged Jh.
On July 24, 1863, Benjamin and Mary were dismissed Jg.[13]

References:
1-2, 4, 6-7, 10. HR; p420d.
1, 6, 12. Pennsylvania Archive #5V588, p851 and county records. Reported by Wilma Molsbery; Youngstown, OH. (RGH BK38)
1-2, 6-8, 13. MONTHLY MEETING NOTES; Westland Meeting House, IN; pp631, 718, 821 & 963. (RGH MI1)

Children:
123*Eliza Hawley	b.	28 Dec 1825
124*Sarah Hawley	b.	2 Feb 1828
125*Samuel Davis Hawley	b.	8 May 1830
126*William Hawley	b.	24 Dec 1833
127*Henry C. Hawley	b.	29 Nov 1849

(58) Mary Hawley, daughter of Caleb and Hannah (Batten) Hawley, was born June 19, 1792 in East Bradford Township, Chester County, Pennsylvania, and married December 27, 1821 in Middleton Township, Columbiana County, Ohio, **(128) David Bishop**, son of _____ and _____ (_____) Bishop.
They were Quakers.[12]

References:
1, 6. HR; p420d.
1-2. PEDIGREE CHART; Edna R. Neary; Cedar Rapids, IA; ipo SHF 8 May 1990. (RGH PN2)
1, 6-7, 12. MONTHLY MEETING NOTES; Westland Meeting House, IN; p631. (RGH MI1)

(59) Richard Hawley, son of Caleb and Hannah (Batten) Hawley, was born March 1, 1794 in East Bradford Township, Chester County, Pennsylvania, and married December 3, 1818 in Plainfield

Township, Belmont County, Ohio, **(129) Rachael Paxson**, daughter of Benjamin and Ruth (_____) Paxson. Richard died in Richmond, Wayne County, Indiana.

He was of Richmond, Wayne County, Indiana. She was of Belmont County, Indiana. They were Quakers.[12]

On November 23, 1818, Richard Gct Plainfield Monthly Meeting to marry Rachel Paxton.

On December 3, 1818 Richard son Calib and Hannah of Columbiana County, Ohio, married in Plainfield Meeting House Rachel Paxson daughter of Benjamin and Ruth, Belmont County, Ohio.

On September 20, 1819, Richard Gct Plainfield Monthly Meeting.

On March 23, 1820, Richard and wife Rachel and daughter Ann Gct West Grove Monthly Meeting, Indiana.[13]

On January 1, 1829, disowned from White Water Meeting House, Indiana for denying the divinity of our Lord and Savior, for being out of unity with the Friend's Society, for allowing a marriage of a member of the Society to be accomplished in their home before a justice of the peace and for giving marriage entertainment after.[14]

References:
1, 4, 12. HR; p420d.
1, 6-7, 13. MONTHLY MEETING NOTES; Westland, IA; pp335, 631. (RGH MI1)
1-2. Edna R. Neary; Cedar Rapids, IA to SHF 8 May 1990. (RGH PN2)
1, 14. Robert A. Hawley; West Palm Beach, FL to SHF; Jul 1989. (RGH BK38)

Children:
   130*Ann Hawley   b. 1 Nov 1819

(60) Jessie Hawley, son of Caleb and Hannah (Batten) Hawley, was born February 11, 1796 in East Bradford Township, Chester County, Pennsylvania, and married 1827, **(131) Eliza Brown**, daughter of Joseph and Sarah (_____) Brown. Jessie died July 31, 1880 in Gower Township, Cedar County, Iowa.

They were of Gower Township, Iowa.

On April 21, 1823, Jesse Gct Salem Monthly Meeting.

On May 23, 1823, Rcof Middleton Monthly Meeting, dated April 21, 1823.

In 1826, Jesse Gct Marlborough Monthly Meeting.[12]

References:
1. HR; p420d.
1-2, 4, 6-7. PEDIGREE CHART; Edna Risdom Neary; Cedar Rapids, IA; ipo SHF 8 May 1990. (RGH PN2)
1, 6, 12. MONTHLY MEETING NOTES; Westland Meeting House, IN; p631, 718. (RGH MI1)
1, 6. Robert A. Hawley; West Palm Beach, FL to SHF; Jul 1989. (RGH BK38)

Children:

132*Ella Hawley	b.	5 Feb 1829	
133*Lavinia Hawley	b.	6 Sep 1830	
134*Sarah Hawley	b.	10 Nov 1832	d. 10 Nov 1832
135*Milton Hawley	b.	1 Feb 1834	
136*Richard Hawley	b.	14 May 1836	
137*Elvira Hawley	b.	14 Mar 1838	d. 11 Oct 1928

(61) Elisha Hawley, son of Caleb and Hannah (Batten) Hawley, was born November 21, 1798 in East Bradford Township, Chester County, Pennsylvania. Elisha died June 14, 1884 in Gower Township, Cedar County, Iowa.

He was of Gower Township, Iowa.

On April 21, 1823, Elisha Gct Salem Monthly Meeting.

In 1826, Elisha Gct Marlborough Monthly Meeting.[12]

References:
1-2. PEDIGREE CHART; Edna R. Neary; Cedar Rapids, IA; ipo SHF 8 May 1990. (RGH PN2)
1, 12. MONTHLY MEETING NOTES; Westland Meeting House, IN; pp631 & 718. (RGH MI1)

(62) Thomas Hawley, son of Caleb and Hannah (Batten) Hawley, was born 1802 in Westland Township, Washington County, Pennsylvania.

References:
1-2. Robert A. Hawley; West Palm Beach, FL to SHF; Jul 1989. (RGH BK38)

(63) Hannah Hawley, daughter of Caleb and Hannah (Batten) Hawley, was born 1804 in Middleton Township, Columbiana County, Ohio. Hannah died May 8, 1880 in Gower Township, Cedar County, Iowa.

She was a Quaker.

On April 21, 1823, Hannah, Sr. and Hannah, Jr. Gct Salem Monthly Meeting.

On April 23, 1823, Hannah, Sr. and Hannah, Jr. Rocf Middleton Monthly Meeting dated April 21, 1823.

Granted certificate in 1828 to transfer to New Garden Meeting House and in 1835 transfer to Marlborough, Stark County, Ohio.[12]

References:
1-2, 4. Robert A. Hawley; West Palm Beach, FL to SHF; Jul 1989. **(RGH BK38)**
1, 12. MONTHLY MEETING NOTES; Westland, IN; pp631 & 718. (RGH MI1)

(65) Mary Hawley, daughter of Joseph and Rebecca (Meredith) Hawley, was born 1799 in West Chester, Chester County, Pennsylvania. Mary died 1822.

References:
1-2, 4. HR; p421a.

(66) Simon Hawley, son of Joseph and Rebecca (Meredith) Hawley, was born 1801 and married 1824, **(138)** _____ _____, daughter of _____ and _____ (_____) _____. Simon died 1863. _____ died 1877.

References:
1-2, 4, 6-7, 10. HR; p421a.

Children:

139*Joseph Hawley	b.	1825
140*Catherine Hawley	b.	1828
141*Albert Hawley	b.	1830
142*Rebecca Hawley	b.	1833
143*Jesse Hawley	b.	1836
144*Amanda Hawley	b.	1839
145*Lewis Hawley	b.	1842

(67) Benjamin Hawley, son of Joseph and Rebecca (Meredith) Hawley, was born 1803 and married 1837, **(146)** _____ _____, daughter of _____ and _____ (_____) _____. Benjamin died 1850. She was living in 1878.[12]

References:
1-2, 4, 6-7, 12. HR; p421a.

Children:

147*John Hawley	b.	1839
148*Bernard Hawley, 1st Lieut.	b.	1846

(68) Joel Hawley, son of Joseph and Rebecca (Meredith) Hawley, was born October 7, 1804 and married December 11, 1833 in Chester, Chester County, Pennsylvania, **(149) Catharine B. Williamson**, daughter of _____ and _____ (_____) Williamson.

He was a Lawyer and Associate Judge. They were of West Chester, Chester County, Pennsylvania.[12] In 1871, Joel of Uwchlan, Pennsylvania, was elected to succeed Judge Barly, over John Rolston, of Honeybrook, and commissioned by Governor Gery, and held the office until the expiration of his term of five years, on December 4, 1876.[13]

References:
1-2, 6-7, 12. HR; p421a.
1, 13. FC; pp370 & 593. (RGH BK38)

Children:

150*Hannah Mary Hawley	b. 25 Sep 1834		
151*Joseph W. Hawley, Col.	b. 14 Jul 1836	d.	Apr 1863
152*Samuel W. Hawley	b. 10 May 1840		

(69) Jesse Hawley, son of Joseph and Rebecca (Meredith) Hawley, was born February 5, 1806 in Chester, Chester County, Pennsylvania, and married 1828 in Pughtown, Chester County, Pennsylvania, **(153) Esther T. Meredith**, daughter of John and Ann (Mendenhall) Meredith, who was born February 23, 1807. Jesse died 1887. Esther T. died 1900.

They were first cousins of Chester, Pennsylvania. Has marriage 1829.[12]

References:
1-2, 6-7. HR; p421a & b.
1-2, 4, 6-7, 12. CAG; Vol. 4, p688; Vol. 6, pp469-470. (RGH BK90, 92)
1, 6-7. IGI.
1, 6, 8. FC; p656. (RGH BK38)

Children:
```
154*Elizabeth M. Hawley
155*Joseph Hawley
156*Anna Hawley
157*Rebecca Hawley          b.      1841 d.        1915
158*Jesse D. Hawley
159*Phebe Hawley
160*Gertrude R. Hawley
```

(70) **Dinah Hawley**, daughter of Joseph and Rebecca (Meredith) Hawley, married (161) **Charles Moore**, son of _____ and _____ (_____) Moore. Dinah died before 1890. Charles died before 1890.

They were of Chester County, Pennsylvania.[12]

References:
1, 4, 12. HR; pp421a & 576a.

Children:
```
162*Henry J. Moore
163*Richard Moore
164*James M. Moore
165*_____ Moore
166*_____ Moore
```

(72) **Gideon Hawley**, son of Robert and Patience (Yearsley) Hawley. Gideon died in Orleans County, New York.

References:
1, 4. HR; p421b.

(73) Mary Hawley, daughter of Robert and Patience (Yearsley) Hawley. Mary died in Shelby Center, Orleans County, New York.

References:
1, 4. HR; p421b.

(74) Robert Hawley, son of Robert and Patience (Yearsley) Hawley. Robert died in Lockport, Niagara County, New York.

References:
1, 4. HR; p421b.

(75) Enos Hawley, son of Robert and Patience (Yearsley) Hawley, was born June 10, 1799 and married February 21, 1822, **(167) Mary S.** _____, daughter of _____ and _____ (_____) _____, who was born September 9, 1795 in Lycoming County, Pennsylvania. Mary S. died September 9, 1872 in Muncy, Lycoming County, Pennsylvania.

References:
1-2, 6-8, 10. HR; p421b.

Children:

168*Harriet Hawley	b.	1 Jan 1823	
169*Milton Hawley	b.	26 Jun 1825	
170*Robert Hawley	b.	6 Oct 1827	
171*Lucretia M. Hawley	b.	3 Dec 1828	d. 10 Jun 1877
172*Alfred Hawley	b.	10 Dec 1833	

(76) Mary "again" Hawley, daughter of Robert and Patience (Yearsley) Hawley. Mary "again" died in Ohio.

References:
1, 4. HR; p421c.

(77) Hannah Hawley, daughter of Robert and Patience (Yearsley) Hawley. She was of Washington County, Pennsylvania.[12]

References:
1, 12. HR; p421c.

(82) Hannah Hicklin, daughter of Joshua and Tamer (Hawley) Hicklin, married **(173) Joseph Marshall**, son of _____ and _____ (_____) Marshall.

References:
1, 6. Mrs. Albert R. Fisher to Mrs. Edna Neary; 19 May 1962; ipo SHF 8 May 1990. (RGH LT7)

(83) Jesse Hicklin, son of Joshua and Tamer (Hawley) Hicklin, married **(174)** _____ _____, daughter of _____ and _____ (_____) _____.

References:
1, 6. Mrs. Albert R. Fisher to Mrs. Edna Neary; 19 May 1962; ipo SHF 8 May 1990. (RGH LT7)

(86) Mary Hawley, daughter of Benjamin and Deborah (Hoopes) Hawley, was born July 11, 1803 in West Chester, Chester County, Pennsylvania.
She was of Chester County, Pennsylvania.[12]

References:
1-2, 12. IGI.

(88) William Kent, son of Daniel and Esther (Hawley) Kent, was born August 3, 1792 in East Fallowfield, Chester County, Pennsylvania, and married October 21, 1818, **(175) Ann Woodward**, daughter of Thomas and Mary (_____) Woodward, who was born April 9, 1795. William died October 15, 1860. Ann died June 4, 1844 in Upper Oxford, Chester County, Pennsylvania and was buried in Penn's Grove, Chester County, Pennsylvania.

He was of East Fallowfield, Pennsylvania. She was of East Marlborough, Pennsylvania. They were Quakers and were married in East Marlboro Meeting House the first marriage there.[12]

References:
1-2, 4-8, 10-12. FC; p621. (RGH BK38)

(89) Joseph Kent, son of Daniel and Esther (Hawley) Kent, was born June 30, 1794 in East Fallowfield, Chester County, Pennsylvania, and married April 29, 1824, **(176) Maria Jane Cook**, daughter of Samuel and Jane (_____) Cook, who was born November 24, 1803. Joseph died July 13, 1863. Maria Jane died April 25, 1881.

He was of Deer Creek, Harford County, Maryland, She was of York County, Pennsylvania. They were Quakers.[12]

References:
1-2, 4, 6-8, 10, 12. FC; p621. (RGH BK38)

(90) Elizabeth Kent, daughter of Daniel and Esther (Hawley) Kent, was born April 19, 1796 in East Fallowfield, Chester County, Pennsylvania. Elizabeth died August 14, 1848.

She was a Quaker of Chester County, Pennsylvania. She was not married.[12]

References:
1-2, 4, 12. FC; p621. (RGH BK38)

(91) Ann Kent, daughter of Daniel and Esther (Hawley) Kent, was born June 22, 1798 in East Fallowfield, Chester County, Pennsylvania, and married March 16, 1826, **(177) Oliver Furness**, son of _____ and _____ (_____) Furness.

They were Quakers of Chester County, Pennsylvania.[12]

References:
1-2, 6-7, 12. FC; p621. (RGH BK38)

(92) Mary Kent, daughter of Daniel and Esther (Hawley) Kent, was born December 29, 1800 in East Fallowfield, Chester County, Pennsylvania, and married August 17, 1820, **(178) Mahlon Brosius**, son of _____ and _____ (_____) Brosius. They were Quakers of Chester County, Pennsylvania.[12]

References:
1-2, 6-7, 12. FC; p621. (RGH BK38)

(93) Daniel Kent, son of Daniel and Esther (Hawley) Kent, was born February 22, 1803 in East Fallowfield, Chester County, Pennsylvania, and married September 16, 1829 in Londonderry, Chester County, Pennsylvania, **(179) Sarah Brosius**, daughter of Henry and Mary (_____) Brosius, who was born October 22, 1808.

He was of East Fallowfield, Chester County, Pennsylvania. She was of Upper Oxford, Chester County, Pennsylvania. They were Quakers and were married at Doe Run Meeting.[12]

References:
1-2, 6-8, 12. FC; p621. (RGH BK38)

(94) Benjamin Kent, son of Daniel and Esther (Hawley) Kent, was born March 23, 1805 and married December 17, 1829, **(180) Hannah Simmons**, daughter of Henry and Rachel (Preston) Simmons, who was born February 18, 1806. Benjamin died 1881.

They were Quakers of Chester County, Pennsylvania.[12]

References:
1-2, 6-8, 12. FC; p621. (RGH BK38)
1-2, 4, 6, 12. CAG; Vol. 1, p174. (RGH BK87)

(98) _____ Hawley, son of Joseph, Jr., and Elizabeth (Woodward) Hawley, was of West Chester, Pennsylvania.[12]

References:
1, 12. HR; p421c.
1. FC; p593. (RGH BK38)

(99) _____ Hawley, son of Joseph, Jr., and Elizabeth (Woodward) Hawley, was of West Chester, Pennsylvania.[12]

References:
1, 12. HR; p421c.

SIXTH GENERATION

(102) Edward [Emanuel] D. Hawley, son of Nathan and Hannah (Eveson) Hawley, was born October 25, 1808 and married October 11, 1832 in Columbiana County, Ohio, **(181) Mary Ann McBride**, daughter of _____ and _____ (_____) McBride. They were Quakers.[12]

References:
1-2, 6. Ruama (Coit) Hawley; Tulsa, OK to SHF 2 Aug 1967. (RGH PN1)
1, 6-7, 12. IGI.

(103) Milton Hawley, son of Nathan and Hannah (Eveson) Hawley, was born February 22, 1810.
He was twin to Mellon.[12]

References:
1-2, 12. Ruama (Coit) Hawley; Tulsa, OK to SHF 2 Aug 1967. (RGH PN1)

(104) Mellon Hawley, son of Nathan and Hannah (Eveson) Hawley, was born February 22, 1810.
He was twin to Milton.[12]

References:
1-2, 12. Ruama (Coit) Hawley; Tulsa, OK to SHF 2 Aug 1967. (RGH PN1)

(105) Calib Hawley, son of Nathan and Hannah (Eveson) Hawley, was born January 2, 1812 and married November 11, 1835 in Columbiana, Columbiana County, Ohio, **(182) Hannah Ball**, daughter of _____ and _____ (_____) Ball, who was born 1815. Hannah died 1865.

Caleb lived on a farm in the small village of Guilford near Lisbon, Columbiana County, Ohio where his children were born. He did some farming, also merchandizing, and for awhile ran a sawmill. They were Quakers.[12]

References:
1-2, 6, 8, 10, 12. Robert A. Hawley; West Palm Beach, FL to SHF; Jul 1989. (RGH BK38)
1, 6-7. IGI.

Children:

183*James Graham Hawley	b.	1836
184*Thomas L. Hawley, Capt.	b.	1838
185*Emanuel Hawley	b.	1840
186*Cicero Stoner Hawley	b.	4 Feb 1842
187*Matilde Hawley		
188*Joseph Hawley	b.	1848
189*Josephine Hawley		
190*Nathan C. Hawley	b.	1850
191*Francis [Frank] M. Hawley	b.	1853
192*Mary V. Hawley	b.	1856

(106) **Aaron Hawley**, son of Nathan and Hannah (Eveson) Hawley, was born February 2, 1814.
He was not married.[12]

References:
1-2, 12. Ruama (Coit) Hawley; Tulsa, OK to SHF 2 Aug 1967. (RGH PN1)

(107) **Jesse Hawley**, son of Nathan and Hannah (Eveson) Hawley, was born August 1, 1816 and married November 3, 1842 in Columbiana County, Ohio, (193) **Adeline Windle**, daughter of _____ and _____ (_____) Windle.

References:
1-2, 6. Ruama (Coit) Hawley; Tulsa, OK to SHF 2 Aug 1967. (RGH PN1)
1, 6-7. IGI.

(108) **Mary Hawley**, daughter of Nathan and Hannah (Eveson) Hawley, was born December 25, 1819 and married July 21, 1839 in Columbiana County, Ohio, (194) **John [Hall] W. Chapman**, son of _____ and _____ (_____) Chapman.

References:
1-2, 6. Ruama (Coit) Hawley; Tulsa, OK to SHF 2 Aug 1967. (RGH PN1)
1, 6-7. IGI.

(109) Benjamin Hawley, son of Nathan and Hannah (Eveson) Hawley, was born October 23, 1821 and married October 16, 1850 in Columbiana County, Ohio, **(195) Elizabeth [Hester] Heston**, daughter of _____ and _____ (_____) Heston.

References:
1-2, 6. Ruama (Coit) Hawley; Tulsa, OK to SHF 2 Aug 1967. (RGH PN1)
1, 6-7. IGI.

Children:
196*Eldora Hawley   b. 9 May 1867 d.   7 Mar 1949

(110) Cynthia Hawley, daughter of Nathan and Hannah (Eveson) Hawley, was born October 12, 1823.

References:
1-2. Ruama (Coit) Hawley; Tulsa, OK to SHF 2 Aug 1967. (RGH PN1)

(111)Jane Hawley, daughter of Nathan and Hannah (Eveson) Hawley, was born March 20, 1826 and married February 3, 1848 in Columbiana County, Ohio, **(197) Caleb Windle**, son of _____ and _____ (_____) Windle.

References:
1-2, 6. Ruama (Coit) Hawley; Tulsa, OK to SHF 2 Aug 1967. (RGH PN1)
1, 6-7. IGI.

(114) Joseph Hawley, son of Caleb, Jr., and Catharine (James) Hawley, was born June 30, 1818 in Elkrun Township, Columbiana County, Ohio, and married about 1840 in Columbiana County, Ohio, **(198) Alice Grewell**, daughter of Timothy and Alice [Pinnock] (Pennock) Grewell, who was born September 11, 1821 in Columbiana County, Ohio. Joseph died December 11, 1905 in Gower Township, Cedar County, Iowa and was buried in Honey Grove Cemetery, Gower Township, Cedar County, Iowa. Alice died July 4, 1897 in Gower Township, Cedar County, Iowa and was buried in Honey Grove Cemetery, Gower Township, Cedar County, Iowa.

He was a Farmer. They were Quakers of Gower Township, Cedar County, Iowa. She is a twin to Ann.

They were living in Marlborough Township, Stark County, Ohio in 1850.[13]

The family migrated to Iowa in 1852 and settled in Cedar County, Iowa. On November 12, 1852 Joseph purchased 160 acres of land from the United States Government in Section 33 in Gower Township. Land price was not listed. During the next few years he also purchased nine other sections of land adjoining his in Gower Township, plus a full section in Springdale Township, Iowa.[12]

References:
1-2. MONTHLY MEETING NOTES; Westland Meeting House, IN; p871. (RGH MI1)
1-2, 6, 7, 13. 1850 Federal Census; Marlborough Township, Stark County, OH. (RGH LT2)
1, 12. Robert A. Hawley; West Palm Beach, FL to SHF; Jul 1989. (RGH LT2)

Children:

199*Isaac Hawley	b.	1841		
200*Alice Hawley	b.	1843		
201*Catharine Hawley	b.	1845		
202*William Hawley	b.	1847	d.	15 Sep 1897
203*Sarah Hawley	b.	1848		
204*Elvin Reece Hawley	b.	19 Jun 1860	d.	7 Jul 1928

(115) **Benjamin Hawley**, son of Caleb, Jr., and Catharine (James) Hawley, was born May 20, 1820 in Sandy Spring Township, Columbiana County, Ohio. Benjamin died June 20, 1894 in West Branch, Cedar County, Iowa. He was a Farmer and Quaker of West Branch, Cedar County, Iowa.[12]

References:
1-2, 4, 12. Robert A. Hawley; West Palm Beach, FL to SHF; Jul 1989. (RGH BK38)

(116) **Phebe Ann Hawley**, daughter of Caleb, Jr., and Catharine (James) Hawley, was born September 3, 1822 in Whitewater Township, Wayne County, Indiana.

She was a Quaker.[12]

References:
1-2, 12. MONTHLY MEETING NOTES; Westland Meeting House, IN; p871. (RGH MI1)

(117) James G. Hawley, son of Caleb, Jr., and Catharine (James) Hawley, was born December 10, 1825 in Carmel Township, Columbiana County, Ohio, and married February 23, 1851 in Portage, Wood County, Ohio, **(205) Mary B. Bishop**, daughter of _____ and _____ (_____) Bishop. James G. died September 3, 1917 in West Branch, Cedar County, Iowa.
They were Quakers.[12]

References:
1-2,.12. MONTHLY MEETING NOTES; Westland Meeting House, IN; p871. (RGH MI1)
1-2, 6-7. IGI.
1-2, 4. Robert A. Hawley; West Palm Beach, FL to SHF; Jul 1989. (RGH BK38)

Children:

206*Byron Hawley	b. 10 Feb 1852
207*Thomas P. Hawley	b. 8 Apr 1854
208*William B. Hawley	b. 22 Sep 1857
209*James Melville Hawley	b. 24 Jun 1870

(118) Latham Hawley, son of Caleb, Jr., and Catharine (James) Hawley, was born October 7, 1827 in Carmel Township, Columbiana County, Ohio. Latham died June 10, 1905 in Gower Township, Cedar County, Iowa.
He was a Quaker.[12]

References:
1-2, 12. MONTHLY MEETING NOTES; Westland Meeting House, IN; p871. (RGH MI1)
1, 4. Robert A. Hawley; West Palm Beach, FL to SHF; Jul 1989. (RGH BK38)

(119) Caleb P. Hawley, son of Caleb, Jr., and Catharine (James) Hawley, was born February 10, 1829 in Carmel Township, Columbiana County, Ohio.
He was a Quaker.[12]

References:
1-2, 12. MONTHLY MEETING NOTES; Westland Meeting House, IN; p871. (RGH NI1)

(120) Sarah Hawley, daughter of Caleb, Jr., and Catharine (James) Hawley, was born March 1, 1833 in Marlborough Township, Stark County, Ohio. Sarah died October 9, 1895 in Gower Township, Cedar County, Iowa.
She was a Quaker.[12]

References:
1-2, 12. MONTHLY MEETING NOTES; Westland Meeting House, IN; p871. (RGH MI1)
1-2, 4. Robert A. Hawley; West Palm Beach, FL to SHF; Jul 1989. (RGH BK38)

(123) Eliza Hawley, daughter of Benjamin and Mary (Davis) Hawley, was born December 28, 1825 in Salem Township, Columbiana County, Ohio, and married February 15, 1846 in Columbiana County, Ohio, **(210) Isaac G. Thomas**, son of _____ and _____ (_____) Thomas.
They were Quakers. On December 23, 1846 Eliza (Hawley) Thomas Con Med.[12]

References:
1, 6-7, 12. HR; p420d.
1-2, 12. MONTHLY MEETING NOTES; Westland Meeting House, IN; p718. (RGH MI1)

Children:
211*	_____	Thomas
212*	_____	Thomas
213*	_____	Thomas
214*	_____	Thomas

(124) Sarah Hawley, daughter of Benjamin and Mary (Davis) Hawley, was born February 2, 1828 in Salem Township, Columbiana County, Ohio, and married June 2, 1853, **(215) Robert B. Hiddleson**, son of _____ and _____ (_____) Hiddleson. Robert B. died October 1, 1858.
They were Quakers.[12]

References:
1, 6-7, 10. HR; p420d.
1-2, 12. MONTHLY MEETING NOTES; Westland Meeting House, IN; p718. (RGH MI1)

(125) Samuel Davis Hawley, son of Benjamin and Mary (Davis) Hawley, was born May 8, 1830 in Salem Township, Columbiana County, Ohio, and married April 27, 1856, **(216) Susan Altemus**, daughter of _____ and _____ (_____) Altemus.
They were Quakers of Philadelphia, Delaware County, Pennsylvania.[12]

References:
1-2, 6-7, 12. HR; p420d.
6, 8. MONTHLY MEETING NOTES; Westland Meeting House, IN; p718. (RGH MI1)

(126) William Hawley, son of Benjamin and Mary (Davis) Hawley, was born December 24, 1833 in Salem Township, Columbiana County, Ohio. He was a Seaman and Quaker. He was lost at sea.[12]

References:
1-2, 12. MONTHLY MEETING NOTES; Westland Meeting House, IN; p718. (RGH MI1)

(127) Henry C. Hawley, son of Benjamin and Mary (Davis) Hawley, was born November 29, 1849.
He was a Quaker of Salem, Columbiana County, Ohio.[12]

References:
1-2, 12. HR; p420d.
1-2, 12. 1850 CENSUS; Perry Township Columbiana County, OH.

(130) Ann Hawley, daughter of Richard and Rachael (Paxson) Hawley, was born November 1, 1819 in Hopewell, Henry County, Indiana.
She was a Quaker of Richmond, Wayne County, Indiana.

On March 23, 1820, Richard and wife Rachel and daughter Ann Get West Grove Meeting House, Indiana.[12]

References:
1, 12. MONTHLY MEETING NOTES; Westland Meeting House, IN; p335. (RGH MI1)

(132) Ella Hawley, daughter of Jessie and Eliza (Brown) Hawley, was born February 5, 1829 and married **(217) Elijah Wherry**, son of _____ and _____ (_____) Wherry.
They were Quakers.[12]

References:
1-2, 6, 12. PEDIGREE CHART; Edna R. Neary; Cedar Rapids, IA; ipo SHF 8 May 1990. (RGH PN2)

Children:
218*Julian Wherry

(133) Lavinia Hawley, daughter of Jessie and Eliza (Brown) Hawley, was born September 6, 1830.
She was a Quaker.[12]

References:
1-2, 12. PEDIGREE CHART; Edna R. Neary; Cedar Rapids, IA.; ipo SHF 8 May 1990. (RGH PN2)

(134) Sarah Hawley, daughter of Jessie and Eliza (Brown) Hawley, was born November 10, 1832. Sarah died November 10, 1832.
She was a Quaker.[12]

References:
1-2, 4, 12. PEDIGREE CHART; Edna R. Neary; Cedar Rapids, IA; ipo SHF 8 May 1990. (RGH PN2)

(135) Milton Hawley, son of Jessie and Eliza (Brown) Hawley, was born February 1, 1834.
He was a Quaker.[12]

References:
1-2, 12. PEDIGREE CHART; Edna R. Neary; Cedar Rapids, IA; ipo SHF 8 May 1990. (RGH PN2)

(136) Richard Hawley, son of Jessie and Eliza (Brown) Hawley, was born May 14, 1836 and married **(219) Flava** _____, daughter of _____ and _____ (_____) _____.
They were Quakers.[12]

References:
1-2, 6, 12. PEDIGREE CHART; Edna R. Neary; Cedar Rapids, IA; ipo SHF 8 May 1990. (RGH PN2)

Children:
220*Theordore Hawley
221*Irvin Hawley

(137) Elvira Hawley, daughter of Jessie and Eliza (Brown) Hawley, was born March 14, 1838 and married February 16, 1860, **(222) Thomas Maudlin**, son of _____ and _____ (_____) Maudlin. Elvira died October 11, 1928.
They were Quakers.[12]

References:
1-2, 4, 6-7, 12. PEDIGREE CHART; Edna R. Neary; Cedar Rapids, IA; ipo SHF 8 May 1990. (RGH PN2)

Children:
223*Ella Maudlin
224*Sylvester Maudlin
225*Mary Maudlin
226*Thomas Maudlin
227*Adora Maudlin
228*Jesse Maudlin
229*Lucinda Maudlin
230*Rethia Maudlin
231*Bertha Maudlin

(139) Joseph Hawley, son of Simon and _____ (_____) Hawley, was born 1825 and married **(232)** _____ _____, daughter of _____ and _____ (_____) _____.

References:
1-2. HR; p421a.

Children:
233*Joseph Hawley
234*Edward B. Hawley   b.c   1846

(140) Catherine Hawley, daughter of Simon and _____ (_____)
Hawley, was born 1828 and married **(235)** _____ **Raper**, Dr., son
of _____ and _____ (_____) Raper.
He was a Physician of Lycoming County, Pennsylvania.[12]

References:
1-2, 6, 12. HR; p421a.

(141) Albert Hawley, son of Simon and _____ (_____)
Hawley, was born 1830 and married **(236)** _____ _____,
daughter of _____ and _____ (_____) _____.
They were of Pottsville, Pennsylvania.[12]

References:
1-2, 6, 12. HR; p421a.

Children:
237*_____ Hawley
238*_____ Hawley
239*_____ Hawley

(142) Rebecca Hawley, daughter of Simon and _____ (_____)
Hawley, was born 1833.
She was not married in 1878.[12]

References:
1-2, 12. HR; p421a.

(143) Jesse Hawley, son of Simon and _____ (_____) Hawley,
was born 1836.
He was not married in 1878.[12]

References:
1-2, 12. HR; p421a.

(144) **Amanda Hawley**, daughter of Simon and _____ (_____)
Hawley, was born 1839.
She was not married in 1878.[12]

References:
1-2, 12. HR; p421a.

(145) **Lewis Hawley**, son of Simon and _____ (_____) Hawley,
was born 1842 and married (240) _____ _____, daughter of
_____ and _____ (_____) _____.
References:
1-2. HR; p421a.

Children:
```
241*_____   Hawley
242*_____   Hawley
```

(147) **John Hawley**, son of Benjamin and _____ (_____)
Hawley, was born 1839.
   Corporal in his brother's, [Lieut. Bernard], Company H, 43rd
Regiment, Pennsylvania [ninety days] Militia. Mustered in July 6,
1863; Discharged August 13, 1863.[12]

References:
1-2. HR; p421a.
1, 12. FC; Appendix pages xxiv & xxxvi. (RGH BK38)

(148) **Bernard Hawley**, 1st Lieut., son of Benjamin and _____
(_____) Hawley, was born 1846.
   He was a Private in Company A [nine months service], 124th
Regiment Infantry in command of Col. Joseph W. Hawley his first
cousin. Mustered in August 8, 1862, mustered out May 17, 1863.
   First Lieutenant in Company H, 43rd Regiment, Pennsylvania
[ninety days] Militia. Mustered in July 6, 1863; Discharged August
13, 1863.[12]

References:
1-2. HR; p421a.
1, 12. FC; ppxxiv & xxxvi. (RGH BK38)

(150) Hannah Mary Hawley, daughter of Joel and Catharine B. (Williamson) Hawley, was born September 25, 1834 and married **(243)** _____ _____, son of _____ and _____ (_____) _____.

She was of Oxford, Pennsylvania. She was living in 1878.[12]

References:
1-2, 12. HR; p421b.

Children:
    244*_____ _____
    245*_____ _____
    246*_____ _____

(151) Joseph W. Hawley, Col., son of Joel and Catharine B. (Williamson) Hawley, was born July 14, 1836 and married **(247)** _____ _____, daughter of _____ and _____ (_____) _____. Joseph W., Col., died April 1863 in Chancellorville, Geneva County, Alabama.

He was a Bank Cashier of Media, Pennsylvania.[12] CIVIL WAR: Member, One Hundred and Twenty-Fourth Regiment, Pennsylvania Volunteers. Companies A,C,E,F.G.H.I. and K, were recruited in Chester County, Pennsylvania, and three Companies in Delaware County. They rendezvoused at Camp Curten near Harrisburg, but before an organization could be affected, they were ordered to Washington, DC and proceeded thither August 12, 1862, under the command of Senior Captain Joseph W. Hawley. Upon their arrival they went into camp near Fort Albany and on the 17th, the regimental organization was effected. This regiment, thought but a brief period in service (nine months), made an honorable history, and was nobly engaged in two great battles--Antietam in September 1862, and Chancellorsville in April and May following. At the former it lost fifty killed and wounded, and of the latter was Colonel Hawley, it's commander. This regiment was mustered out May 17, 1863 at Harrisburg.[13]

References:
1-2, 6, 12. HR; p421b.
1, 4, 13. FC; p142. (RGH BK38)

(152) Samuel W. Hawley, son of Joel and Catharine B. (Williamson) Hawley, was born May 10, 1840.

References:
1-2. HR; p421b.

(154) Elizabeth M. Hawley, daughter of Jesse and Esther T. (Meredith) Hawley.

References:
1. HR; p421b.

(155) Joseph Hawley, son of Jesse and Esther T. (Meredith) Hawley, married **(248)** _____ _____, daughter of _____ and _____ (_____) _____.

References:
1, 6. HR; p421b.

(156) Anna Hawley, daughter of Jesse and Esther T. (Meredith) Hawley.

References:
1. HR; p421b.

(157) Rebecca Hawley, daughter of Jesse and Esther T. (Meredith) Hawley, was born 1841 in Pughtown, Chester County, Pennsylvania, and married 1866/1867 in Norristown, Montgomery County, Pennsylvania, **(249) William Dell Reinhardt, Dr.**, son of _____ and _____ (_____) Reinhardt, who was born 1830. Rebecca died 1915. William Dell, Dr., died 1880.
    She was of Pughtown, Pennsylvania. He was a Physician of Marietta,
Pennsylvania, a Graduate of University of Pennsylvania 1852.[12]

References:
1. HR; p421b.
1-2, 4, 6-7, 12. CAG; Vol. 4, p688; Vol. 6, pp469-470. (RGH BK90,92)

Children:

250*David Jones Reinhardt	b.	6 Nov 1867	d.	22 Nov 1935
251*Jesse Hawley Reinhardt	b.	1869		
252*Mary B. Reinhardt	b.	1870		
253*Esther Meredith Reinhardt	b.	1872		
254*Lydia Ludwig Reinhardt	b.	1875		
255*Elizabeth C. Reinhardt	b.	1877		

(158) Jesse D. Hawley, son of Jesse and Esther T. (Meredith) Hawley, married **(256)** _____ _____, daughter of _____ and _____ (_____) _____.

He was Editor and Proprietor of the Eagle, Reading, Pennsylvania.[12]

References:
1, 6, 12. HR; p421b.

(159) Phebe Hawley, daughter of Jesse and Esther T. (Meredith) Hawley.
References:
1. HR; p421b.

(160) Gertrude R. Hawley, daughter of Jesse and Esther T. (Meredith) Hawley, married **(257)** _____ _____, son of _____ and _____ (_____) _____.

References:
1, 6. HR; p421b.

(162) Henry J. Moore, son of Charles and Dinah (Hawley) Moore.

References:
1. HR; p576a.

(163) Richard Moore, son of Charles and Dinah (Hawley) Moore.

References:
1. HR; p576a.

(164) James M. Moore, son of Charles and Dinah (Hawley) Moore.

References:
1. HR; p576a.

(165) _____ Moore, child of Charles and Dinah (Hawley) Moore.

_____ died early.[12]

References:
1, 12. HR; p576a.

(166) _____ Moore, child of Charles and Dinah (Hawley) Moore.

_____ died early.[12]

References:
1, 12. HR; p576a.

(168) Harriet Hawley, daughter of Enos and Mary S. (_____)
Hawley, was born January 1, 1823.

References:
1-2. HR; p421b.

(169) Milton Hawley, son of Enos and Mary S. (_____) Hawley,
was born June 26, 1825 and married September 1848, **(258) Jane L.
Alder**, daughter of _____ and _____ (_____) Adler.

References:
1-2, 6-7. HR; pp421b, c.

(170) **Robert Hawley**, son of Enos and Mary S. (_____) Hawley, was born October 6, 1827 and married June 11, 1856 in Muncy, Lycoming County, Pennsylvania, (261) **Sarah Jane Cooke**, daughter of _____ and _____ (_____) Cooke.
They were of Muncy, Pennsylvania.[12]

References:
1-2, 6-7, 12. HR; pp421b, c.

Children:

262*Madge Hawley	b. 2 Sep 1857
263*William Enos Hawley	b. 24 Feb 1860
264*James Dobbins Hawley	b. 17 Oct 1863

(171) **Lucretia M. Hawley**, daughter of Enos and Mary S. (_____) Hawley, was born December 3, 1828. Lucretia M. died June 10, 1877 in Muncy, Lycoming County, Pennsylvania.
She was of Muncy, Pennsylvania.[12]

References:
1-2, 4, 12. HR; p421b.

(172) **Alfred Hawley**, son of Enos and Mary S. (_____) Hawley, was born December 10, 1833 and married March 23, 1864, (265) Rachel L. Willets, daughter of _____ and _____ (_____) Willets.
They were of Northumberland, Pennsylvania.[12]

References:
1-2, 6-7, 12. HR; p421c.

SEVENTH GENERATION

(183) James Graham Hawley, son of Calib and Hannah (Ball) Hawley, was born 1836 and married **(266) Louise Farrar**, daughter of _____ and _____ (_____) Farrar.
They were of Albuquerque[12] and Santa Fe, New Mexico.[13]

References:
1-2, 13. 1850 CENSUS Hanover Township, Columbiana County, OH.
1-2, 12. Ruama (Coit) Hawley; Tulsa, OK to SHF 2 Aug 1967. (RGH PN1)

(184) Thomas Leonard Hawley, Capt., son of Calib and Hannah (Ball) Hawley, was born 1838. Thomas Leonard, Capt., died in Andersonville, Sumpter County, Georgia.
He was a Captain in the United States Army in the Civil War. Died of tuberculosis while a prisoner at Andersonville.[12]

References:
1-2. 1850 CENSUS Hanover Township, Columbiana County, OH.
1, 12. Ruama (Coit) Hawley; Tulsa, OK to SHF; 2 Aug 1967. (RGH PN1)

(185) Emanuel Hawley, son of Calib and Hannah (Ball) Hawley, was born 1840 and married March 28, 1863 in Columbiana, Columbiana County, Ohio, **(267) Kate B. Ask**, daughter of _____ and _____ (_____) Ask.
Emanuel worked in a bank, he was a Quaker. She was of Albuquerque and Santa Fe, New Mexico.[12]

References:
1-2. 1850 CENSUS Hanover Township, Columbiana County, OH.
1, 6-7, 12. IGI.

(186) Cicero Stoner Hawley, son of Calib and Hannah (Ball) Hawley, was born February 4, 1842 and married 1871 in Marshalltown, Marshall County, Iowa, **(268) Lyra Belle Shaw**, daughter of _____ and _____ (_____) Shaw.

He was a Quaker. She was of Albuquerque and Santa Fe, New Mexico.

Cicero learned the printers trade in Salem, Ohio about 10 miles from Guilford.

He enlisted for the war in 1861 at the age of 18 and served to the end with the 104th Ohio Infantry. At one point, for a month or so, he was put in charge of an abandoned Confederate newspaper and ran it for the Union forces. After the war, he got a job on a newspaper in Marshalltown, Iowa where he met and married Lyra Belle Shaw. Soon after their marriage, they decided to journey to southern California. Other Iowa friends [the Giddings family)]had already settled in Indiana Colony, which later became Pasadena. All of their children were born in California.

References:
1-2. Robert A. Hawley; West Palm Beach, FL to SHF; Jul 1989. (RGH BK38)
1-2. 1850 CENSUS Hanover Township, Columbiana County, OH.
6-8. Ruama (Coit) Hawley; Tulsa, OK to SHF 2 Aug 1967. (RGH PN1)

Children:

269*Fred Graham Hawley	b. 14 Nov 1874	d. 11 Jul 1962
270*Agnes Genevieve Hawley	b. 4 Nov 1878	d.	Jan 1966
271*Walter Eastman Hawley	b. 13 Nov 1881	
272*Frank Lawrence Hawley	b. 7 Sep 1886	d.c	1950
273*Helen Margaret Hawley	b. 3 May 1890	d.c	1895

(187) **Matilde Hawley**, daughter of Calib and Hannah (Ball) Hawley, was a Quaker. She died young.[12]

References:
1, 12. Robert A. Hawley; West Palm Beach, FL to SHF; Jul 1989. (RGH BK38)

(188) **Joseph Hawley**, son of Calib and Hannah (Ball) Hawley, was born 1848.

He was a Quaker.[12]

References:
1-2, 12. 1850 CENSUS Hanover Township, Columbiana County, OH.

(189) Josephine Hawley, daughter of Calib and Hannah (Ball) Hawley, married (274) Martin Crosser, son of _____ and _____ (_____) Crosser.
They were Quakers.[12]

References:
1, 6, 12. Robert A. Hawley; West Palm Beach, FL to SHF; Jul 1989. (RGH BK38)

(190) Nathan C. Hawley, son of Calib and Hannah (Ball) Hawley, was born 1850 and married October 22, 1873 in Ashtabula, Ashtabula County, Ohio, (275) Stella Jane Hill, daughter of _____ and _____ (_____)
Hill.
They were Quakers. Nathan worked in the United States Government Printing Office in Washington, DC.[12]

References:
1-2. 1860 CENSUS Columbiana, OH.
1, 6-7. IGI.
1, 12. Ruama (Coit) Hawley; Tulsa, OK to SHF; 2 Aug 1967. (RGH PN1)

Children:
276*Bertha Hawley   b. 24 Jul 1875

(191) Francis [Frank] M. Hawley, son of Calib and Hannah (Ball) Hawley, was born 1853 and married November 4, 1879 in Columbiana, Columbiana County, Ohio, (277) Bell C. Adams, daughter of _____ and _____ (_____) Adams.
They were Quakers. Frank edited the Wellesville Union newspaper and in later years worked in the United States Government Printing Office in Washington, DC.[12]

References:
1-2. 1860 CENSUS Columbiana, OH.
1, 6-7. IGI.
1, 6, 12. Ruama (Coit) Hawley; Tulsa, OK to SHF; 2 Aug 1967. (RGH PN1)

He also married (278) Margaret McDonald, daughter of _____
and _____ (_____) McDonald.

References:
1, 6. Ruama (Coit) Hawley; Tulsa, OK to SHF; 2 Aug 1967. (RGH PN1)

(192) Mary V. Hawley, daughter of Calib and Hannah (Ball)
Hawley, was born 1856 and married April 11, 1877 in Columbiana,
Columbiana County, Ohio, (279) Elmore J. Ingram, son of
_____ and _____ (_____) Ingram.
They were Quakers.[12]

References:
1-2, 12. 1860 CENSUS Columbiana, OH.
1, 6-7. IGI.

(196) Eldora Hawley, daughter of Benjamin and Elizabeth [Hester]
(Heston) Hawley, was born May 9, 1867 in Monmouth, Warren
County, Illinois, and married March 1885, (280) John Byron Hays,
son of _____ and _____ (_____) Hays. Eldora died March
7, 1949 in Lincoln, Lancaster County, Nebraska and was buried in
Smith Center, Smith County, Kansas.

References:
1-2, 4-7. IGI.

She also married (281) _____ Jahnke, son of _____ and
_____ (_____) Jahnke.

References:
1, 6. IGI.

(199) Isaac Hawley, son of Joseph and Alice (Grewell) Hawley, was
born 1841 in Marlborough Township, Stark County, Ohio.

References:
1-2. Robert A. Hawley; West Palm Beach, FL to SHF; Jul 1989. (RGH BK38)

(200) Alice Hawley, daughter of Joseph and Alice (Grewell) Hawley, was born 1843 in Marlborough Township, Stark County, Ohio.

References:
1-2. Robert A. Hawley; West Palm Beach, FL to SHF; Jul 1989. (RGH BK38)

(201) Catharine Hawley, daughter of Joseph and Alice (Grewell) Hawley, was born 1845 in Marlborough Township, Stark County, Ohio.

References:
1-2. Robert A. Hawley; West Palm Beach, FL to SHF; Jul 1989. (RGH BK38)

(202) William Hawley, son of Joseph and Alice (Grewell) Hawley, was born 1847 in Marlborough Township, Stark County, Ohio. William died September 15, 1897 in Gower Township, Cedar County, Iowa.
He was of Cower Township, Cedar County, Iowa.[12]

References:
1-2, 4, 12. Robert A. Hawley; West Palm Beach, FL to SHF; Jul 1989. (RGH BK38)

(203) Sarah Hawley, daughter of Joseph and Alice (Grewell) Hawley, was born 1848 in Marlborough Township, Stark County, Ohio.

References:
1-2. Robert A. Hawley; West Palm Beach, FL to SHF; Jul 1989. (RGH BK38)

(204) Elvin Reece Hawley, son of Joseph and Alice (Grewell) Hawley, was born June 19, 1860 in West Branch, Cedar County, Iowa, and married March 27, 1879 in West Branch, Cedar County, Iowa, **(282) Elnora Bell**, daughter of John W. and Elizabeth (Hoffman) Bell, who was born February 20, 1861 in West Branch, Cedar County, Iowa. Elvin Reece died July 7, 1928 in Sioux City, Woodbury County, Iowa. Elnora died March 17, 1933 in Sioux City, Woodbury County, Iowa.

They were of Sioux City, Woodbury County, Iowa.[12]

References:
1-2, 4, 6-8, 10, 12. Robert A. Hawley; West Palm Beach, FL to SHF; Jul 1989.
(RGH BK38, FG4)

Children:

283*Orpha Hawley	b. 26 Dec 1879	d.	Nov 1969
284*Alvro N. Hawley	b. 4 Jul 1881	d.	1945
285*John Joseph Hawley	b. 15 Mar 1883	d. 21 Oct 1940	
286*Alice Hawley	b. 2 Aug 1898	d. 24 Nov 1964	
287*Anna Mae Hawley	b. 18 Sep 1899	d. 16 Feb 1925	

(206) **Byron Hawley**, son of James G. and Mary B. (Bishop) Hawley, was born February 10, 1852 in Honey Grove, Cedar County, Iowa.

References:
1-2. IGI.

(207) **Thomas P. Hawley**, son of James G. and Mary B. (Bishop) Hawley, was born April 8, 1854 in Honey Grove, Cedar County, Iowa.

References:
1-2. IGI.

(208) **William B. Hawley**, son of James G. and Mary B. (Bishop) Hawley, was born September 22, 1857 in Honey Grove, Cedar County, Iowa.

References:
1-2. IGI.

(209) **James Melville Hawley**, son of James G. and Mary B. (Bishop) Hawley, was born June 24, 1870 in Honey Grove, Cedar County, Iowa.

References:
1-2. IGI.

(211) _____ **Thomas**, child of Isaac G. and Eliza (Hawley) Thomas, was a Quaker.[12]

References:
1, 12. HR; p420d.

(212) _____ **Thomas**, child of Isaac G. and Eliza (Hawley) Thomas, was a Quaker.[12]

References:
1, 12. HR; p420d.

(213) _____ **Thomas**, child of Isaac G. and Eliza (Hawley) Thomas, was a Quaker.[12]

References:
1, 12. HR; p420d.

(214) _____ **Thomas**, child of Isaac G. and Eliza (Hawley) Thomas, was a Quaker.[12]

References:
1, 12. HR; p420d.

(218) Julian Wherry, son of Elijah and Ella (Hawley) Wherry, was a Quaker.[12]

References:
1, 12. PEDIGREE CHART; Edna R. Neary; Cedar Rapids, IA; ipo SHF 8 May 1990. (RGH PN2)

(220) Theordore Hawley, son of Richard and Flava (_____) Hawley, was a Quaker.[12]

References:
1, 12. PEDIGREE CHART; Edna R. Neary; Cedar Rapids, IA; ipo SHF 8 May 1990. (RGH PN2)

(221) Irvin Hawley, son of Richard and Flava (_____) Hawley, was a Quaker.[12]

References:
1, 12. PEDIGREE CHART; Edna R. Neary; Cedar Rapids, IA; ipo SHF 8 May 1990. (RGH PN2)

(223) Ella Maudlin, daughter of Thomas and Elvira (Hawley) Maudlin, was a Quaker.[12]

References:
1, 12. PEDIGREE CHART; Edna R. Neary; Cedar Rapids, IA; ipo SHF 8 May 1990. (RGH PN2)

(224) Sylvester Maudlin, son of Thomas and Elvira (Hawley) Maudlin, was a Quaker.[12]

References:
1, 12. PEDIGREE CHART; Edna R. Neary; Cedar Rapids, IA; ipo SHF 8 May 1990. (RGH PN2)

(225) Mary Maudlin, daughter of Thomas and Elvira (Hawley) Maudlin, was a Quaker.[12]

References:
1, 12. PEDIGREE CHART; Edna R. Neary; Cedar Rapids, IA; ipo SHF 8 May 1990. (RGH PN2)

(226) Thomas Maudlin, son of Thomas and Elvira (Hawley) Maudlin, was a Quaker.[12]

References:
1, 12. PEDIGREE CHART; Edna R. Neary; Cedar Rapids, IA; ipo SHF 8 May 1990. (RGH PN2)

(227) Adora Maudlin, daughter of Thomas and Elvira (Hawley) Maudlin, was a Quaker.[12]

References:
1, 12. PEDIGREE CHART; Edna R. Neary; Cedar Rapids, IA; ipo SHF 8 May 1990. (RGH PN2)

(228) Jesse Maudlin, son of Thomas and Elvira (Hawley) Maudlin, was a Quaker.[12]

References:
1, 12. PEDIGREE CHART; Edna R. Neary; Cedar Rapids, IA; ipo SHF 8 May 1990. (RGH PN2)

(229) Lucinda Maudlin, daughter of Thomas and Elvira (Hawley) Maudlin, was a Quaker.[12]

References:
1, 12. PEDIGREE CHART; Edna R. Neary; Cedar Rapids, IA; ipo SHF 8 May 1990. (RGH PN2)

(230) Rethia Maudlin, daughter of Thomas and Elvira (Hawley) Maudlin, married **(288) William Risdom**, son of _____ and _____ (_____) Risdom.
They were Quakers.[12]

References:
1, 6, 12. PEDIGREE CHART; Edna R. Neary; Cedar Rapids, IA; ipo SHF 8 May 1990. (RGH PN2)

Children:
289*Edna Risdom

(231) Bertha Maudlin, daughter of Thomas and Elvira (Hawley) Maudlin, was a Quaker.[12]

References:
1, 12. PEDIGREE CHART; Edna R. Neary; Cedar Rapids, IA; ipo SHF 8 May 1990. (RGH PN2)

(233) **Joseph Hawley**, son of Joseph and _____ (_____)
Hawley.

References:
1. HR; p421a.

(234) **Edward B. Hawley**, son of Joseph and _____ (_____)
Hawley, was born about 1846.

He was a Private in Company A (nine months service), 124th
Regiment Infantry in command of Col. Joseph W. Hawley his first
cousin once removed. Mustered in August 8, 1862, mustered out
May 17, 1863.[12]

References:
1. HR; p421a.
1, 12. FC; Appendix page xxiv. (RGH BK38)

(237) _____ **Hawley**, child of Albert and _____ (_____)
Hawley, was of Pottsville, Pennsylvania.[12]

References:
1, 12. HR; p421a.

(238) _____ **Hawley**, child of Albert and _____ (_____)
Hawley, was of Pottsville, Pennsylvania.[12]

References:
1, 12. HR; p421a.

(239) _____ **Hawley**, child of Albert and _____ (_____)
Hawley, was of Pottsville, Pennsylvania.[12]

References:
1, 12. HR; p421a.

(241) _____ **Hawley**, child of Lewis and _____ (_____)
Hawley.

References:
1. HR; p421a.

(242) _____ **Hawley**, child of Lewis and _____ (_____) Hawley.

References:
1. HR; p421a.

(244) _____ _____, daughter of _____ and Hannah Mary (Hawley) _____, was of Oxford, Pennsylvania. She was living in 1878.[12]

References:
1, 12. HR; p421b.

(245) _____ _____, daughter of _____ and Hannah Mary (Hawley) _____, was of Oxford, Pennsylvania. She was living in 1878.[12]

References:
1, 12. HR; p421b.

(246) _____ _____, daughter of _____ and Hannah Mary (Hawley) _____, was of Oxford, Pennsylvania. She was living in 1878.[12]

References:
1, 12. HR; p421b.

(250) David Jones Reinhardt, son of William Dell, Dr., and Rebecca (Hawley) Reinhardt, was born November 6, 1867 in Norristown, Montgomery County, Pennsylvania, and married June 30, 1896, **(290) Anna Margaret Hewes**, daughter of Thomas and Elizabeth Andrews (Miller) Hewes, who was born January 2, 1867 in Salem, Salem County, New Jersey. David Jones died November 22, 1935.

He was a Lawyer. They were of Wilmington, Delaware. He
earned a B.S. at Haverford in 1889. He was a Law Student in Col.
Benjamin Nield's office, 1892-1896. He was a Teacher at Friends'
School, Wilmington, 1889-1894. Admitted to bar, June 1896. City
Solicitor, Wilmington, 1901-1903; member Delaware Senate,
1913-1914; Attorney General of Delaware 1917-1921. Republican,
Clubs: Wilmington, Tuscarora, Little Bushkill Rod and Gun
[Pennsylvania].[12]

References:
1-2, 4, 6-8, 12. CAG; Vol. 4; p688. (RGH BK90)

(251) **Jesse Hawley Reinhardt**, son of William Dell, Dr., and
Rebecca (Hawley) Reinhardt, was born 1869.

References:
1-2. CAG; Vol. 4; p688. (RGH BK90)

(252) **Mary B. Reinhardt**, daughter of William Dell, Dr., and
Rebecca (Hawley) Reinhardt, was born 1870.

References:
1-2. CAG; Vol. 4, p688. (RGH BK90)

(253) **Esther Meredith Reinhardt**, daughter of William Dell, Dr.,
and Rebecca (Hawley) Reinhardt, was born 1872.

References:
1-2. CAG; Vol. 4, p688. (RGH BK90)

(254) **Lydia Ludwig Reinhardt**, daughter of William Dell, Dr., and
Rebecca (Hawley) Reinhardt, was born 1875.

References:
1-2. CAG; Vol. 4, p688. (RGH BK90)

(255) **Elizabeth C. Reinhardt**, daughter of William Dell, Dr., and
Rebecca (Hawley) Reinhardt, was born 1877.

References:
1-2. CAG; Vol. 4, p688. (RGH BK90)

(259) Emma Frances Hawley, daughter of Milton and Jane L. (Alder) Hawley, was baptized April 3, 1863.

References:
1, 3. HR; p421c.

(260) Caroline Lyon Hawley, daughter of Milton and Jane L. (Alder) Hawley, was baptized April 3, 1863.

References:
1, 3, 12. HR; p421c.

(262) Madge Hawley, daughter of Robert and Sarah Jane (Cooke) Hawley, was born September 2, 1857.
She was of Muncy, Pennsylvania.[12]

References:
1-2, 12. HR; p421c.

(263) William Enos Hawley, son of Robert and Sarah Jane (Cooke) Hawley, was born February 24, 1860.
He was of Muncy, Pennsylvania.[12]

References:
1-2, 12. HR; p421c.

(264) James Dobbins Hawley, son of Robert and Sarah Jane (Cooke) Hawley, was born October 17, 1863.
He was of Muncy, Pennsylvania.[12]

References:
1-2, 12. HR; p421c.

EIGHTH GENERATION

(269) **Fred Graham Hawley**, son of Cicero Stoner and Lyra Belle (Shaw) Hawley, was born November 14, 1874 in San Bernardino, San Bernardino Co, California, and married June 9, 1903 in Los Angeles, Los Angeles County, California, (291) **Amy May Roach**, daughter of David Llewellyn and Mary (Morse) Roach. Fred Graham died July 11, 1962 in Tulsa, Tulsa County, Oklahoma. Amy May died 1954.

They were of Albuquerque and Santa Fe, New Mexico.[12]

Fred was educated at the University of Arizona and resided with his wife and children in that state from 1914 to about 1954, the year of his wife's death. He was Chief Chemist for the International Smelting Company, Miami, Arizona. After retirement he was Consulting Chemist for the United States Bureau of Mines, Tucson, Arizona from 1948-1953.

He was a life member of the American Chemical Society for 50 Years of active membership and member of the Arizona Historical Society. Other interests were Archeology, Mineralogy and Cactus culture.

In the fall of 1887 Father and I [Fred Graham Hawley] went East to visit Grandfather Caleb Hawley. We stayed for five days in Chicago with Cary Vaughan, a cousin. Then nearly a month with Grandfather Hawley and Aunt Mary Ingram and her husband at Guilford, Ohio. Aunt Joe Crosser lived in a nearby town. We made side trips to Uncle Nate and his family at Ashtabula, to Uncle Frank Hawley at Wellsville and to Uncle Manuel at Jeffersonville, Indiana. We made the trip to Niagara with Aunt Mary. Uncle Gra' [J. Graham Hawley] returned to California with us.[12]

References:
1-2, 4, 6-7, 10, 12. Ruama (Coit) Hawley; Tulsa, OK to SHF 2 Aug 1967. (RGH PN1)

Children:

```
292*Florence May Hawley, Dr.      b. 17 Sep 1906
293*Paul Frederick Hawley         b. 26 Apr 1910
```

(270) Agnes Genevieve Hawley, daughter of Cicero Stoner and Lyra Belle (Shaw) Hawley, was born November 4, 1878 and married **(294) Forrest M. Whitaker**, son of _____ and _____ (_____) Whitaker. Agnes Genevieve died January 1966. She was of Albuquerque and Santa Fe, New Mexico.[12]

References:
1, 4, 6, 12. Ruama (Coit) Hawley; Tulsa, OK to SHF 2 Aug 1967. (RGH PN1)

(271) Walter Eastman Hawley, son of Cicero Stoner and Lyra Belle (Shaw) Hawley, was born November 13, 1881 in Glendale, Los Angeles County, California, and married **(295) Edith Trout**, daughter of _____ and _____ (_____) Trout.

With his brother Frank, he established the firm of Hawley and Hawley, Assayists, of Douglas and Tucson, Arizona. He resided in Albuquerque and Santa Fe, New Mexico.[12]

References:
1, 6, 12. Ruama (Coit) Hawley; Tulsa, OK to SHF 2 Aug 1967. (RGH PN1)

(272) Frank Lawrence Hawley, son of Cicero Stoner and Lyra Belle (Shaw) Hawley, was born September 7, 1886 in Glendale, Los Angeles County, California. Frank Lawrence died about 1950.

With his brother Walter, he established the firm of Hawley and Hawley, Assayists, of Douglas and Tucson, Arizona. He resided in Albuquerque and Santa Fe, New Mexico.[12]

References:
1, 4, 12. Ruama (Coit) Hawley; Tulsa, OK to SHF 2 Aug 1967. (RGH PN1)

(273) Helen Margaret Hawley, daughter of Cicero Stoner and Lyra Belle (Shaw) Hawley, was born May 3, 1890 in Glendale, Los Angeles County, California, and married **(296) Newel H. Wadsworth**, son of _____ and _____ (_____) Wadsworth. Helen Margaret died about 1895.

They resided in Albuquerque and Santa Fe, New Mexico.[12]

References:
1, 4, 6, 12. Ruama (Coit) Hawley; Tulsa, OK to SHF 2 Aug 1967. (RGH PN1)

(276) **Bertha Hawley**, daughter of Nathan C. and Stella Jane (Hill) Hawley, was born July 24, 1875 in Geneva, Ashtabula County, Ohio.

References:
1-2. IGI.

(283) **Orpha Hawley**, daughter of Elvin Reece and Elnora (Bell) Hawley, was born December 26, 1879 in Kingsley, Plymouth County, Iowa, and married December 27, 1899 in Sioux City, Woodbury County, Iowa, (297) **Charles Hough**, son of _____ and _____ (_____) Hough, who was born in Sioux City, Woodbury County, Iowa. Orpha died November 1969 in Sioux City, Woodbury County, Iowa.
He was a Piano Instructor.[12]

References:
1-2, 4, 6-7, 12. Robert A. Hawley; West Palm Beach, FL to SHF; Jul 1989. (RGH BK38)

Children:
    298*Elvin Hough
    299*Lucille Hough
    300*Gladys Hough

(284) **Alvro N. Hawley**, son of Elvin Reece and Elnora (Bell) Hawley, was born July 4, 1881 in Kingsley, Plymouth County, Iowa, and married March 5, 1881 in Sioux City, Woodbury County, Iowa, (301) **Bessie Lake**, daughter of _____ and _____ (_____) Lake, who was born in Sioux City, Woodbury County, Iowa. Alvro N. died 1945 in Omaha, Douglas County, Nebraska.
He was a Bookkeeper. She was a Sales Clerk. They were of Omaha, Nebraska.[12]

References:
1-2, 4, 6-7, 12. Robert A. Hawley; West Palm Beach, FL to SHF; 3 Apr 1990.
(RGH FG4))

Children:
302*Eugene Hawley
303*Helen Jane Hawley

He also married (304) **Opal Miller**, daughter of _____ and
_____ (_____) Miller.

References:
1, 6. Robert A. Hawley; West Palm Beach, FL to SHF; 3 Apr 1990. (RGH FG4)

(285) **John Joseph Hawley**, son of Elvin Reece and Elnora (Bell)
Hawley, was born March 15, 1883 in Kingsley, Plymouth County,
Iowa, and married May 10, 1904 in Sioux City, Woodbury County,
Iowa, (305) **Cecelia Keeffe**, daughter of Michael and Margaret J.
(Kelly) Keeffe, who was born September 28, 1878 in Sioux City,
Woodbury County, Iowa. John Joseph died October 21, 1940 in
Sioux City, Woodbury County, Iowa. Cecelia died September 10,
1931 in Sioux City, Woodbury County, Iowa.
He was a Livestock Salesman. They were of Sioux City, Iowa.[12]

References:
1-2, 4, 6-8, 10, 12. Robert A. Hawley; West Palm Beach, FL to SHF; Jul 1989.
(RGH BK38)

Children:

306*John Joseph Hawley, Jr.	b.	9 Dec 1905	d.	29 Jan 1952
307*James Hawley	b.	1906	d.	1906
308*Jennette Hawley	b.	28 Jul 1907	d.	30 Apr 1912
309*Marion Hawley	b.	5 Jan 1910	d.	4 Nov 1978
310*Robert A. Hawley	b.	27 Jul 1915	d.	22 Sep 1990

He also married (311) **Ruth Weyenburg**, daughter of _____ and
_____ (_____) Weyenburg.

References:
6. Robert A. Hawley; West Palm Beach, FL to SHF; 3 Apr 1990. (RGH FG4)

(286) Alice Hawley, daughter of Elvin Reece and Elnora (Bell) Hawley, was born August 2, 1898 in Sioux City, Woodbury County, Iowa, and married **(312) Everet Haggard**, son of _____ and _____ (_____) Haggard. Alice died November 24, 1964 in Sioux City, Woodbury County, Iowa.

She was of Sioux City, Iowa. He was a Funeral Director.[12]

References:
1-2, 4, 6. Robert A. Hawley; West Palm Beach, FL to SHF; 3 Apr 1990. (RGH FG4)

Children:
313*Mary Alice Haggard

She also married **(314) Ben Frank**, son of _____ and _____ (_____) Frank.

References:
1, 6. Robert A. Hawley; West Palm Beach, FL to SHF; 3 Apr 1990. (RGH FG4)

(287) Anna Mae Hawley, daughter of Elvin Reece and Elnora (Bell) Hawley, was born September 18, 1899 in Sioux City, Woodbury County, Iowa. Anna Mae died February 16, 1925 in Sioux City, Woodbury County, Iowa.

She was a Clerk of Sioux City, Iowa.[12]

References:
1-2, 4. Robert A. Hawley; West Palm Beach, FL to SHF; Jul 1989. (RGH BK38)

(289) Edna Risdom, daughter of William and Rethia (Maudlin) Risdom, married **(315)** _____ **Neary**, son of _____ and _____ (_____) Neary.

She was of Cedar Rapids, Iowa.[12]

References:
1, 6. PEDIGREE CHART; Edna R. Neary; Cedar Rapids, IA; ipo SHF 8 May 1990. (RGH PN2)

NINTH GENERATION

(292) Florence May Hawley, Dr., daughter of Fred Graham and Amy May (Roach) Hawley, was born September 17, 1906 in Cannanea, Sonora County, Mexico, and married **(316) Bruce Ellis**, son of _____ and _____ (_____) Ellis.

Florence was a well known Anthropologist of the Southwest. She was educated at the University of Arizona and the University of Chicago and became professor of Anthropology at the University of New Mexico. She resided in Albuquerque and Santa Fe, New Mexico.[12]

References:
1-2, 6, 12. Ruama (Coit) Hawley; Tulsa, OK to SHF 2 Aug 1967. (RGH PN1)

Children:
317*Andrea Ellis

(293) Paul Frederick Hawley, son of Fred Graham and Amy May (Roach) Hawley, was born April 26, 1910 in Cannanea, Sonora County, Mexico, and married **(318) Ruhamah [Ruama] Mather Coit**, daughter of Ruel Harlan and Sadie Emmeline (Nutter) Coit, who was born April 26, 1910 in Cannanea, Sonora County, Mexico. Ruhamah [Ruama] Mather died August 20, 1989 in Tulsa, Tulsa County, Oklahoma.

Paul was educated at the University of Arizona and the California Institute of Technology and graduated in 1937 with a Ph.D. in Law and Electrical Engineering. He was an Attorney and Patent Director for Pan American Petroleum Corporation and Lecturer in Physics at the University of Tulsa, Oklahoma. He was a member of the American Bar Association.

They lived in Tulsa, Oklahoma.[12]

References:
1-2, 6-8, 12. Ruama (Coit) Hawley; Tulsa, OK to SHF 2 Aug 1967. (RGH PN1)
6, 10. Paul F. Hawley, Tulsa, OK to SHF. (DMH)

Children:

319*Joyce Lyons Hawley	b. 6 Mar 1942
320*Fred Graham Hawley, II	b. 21 Aug 1945

(298) **Elvin Hough**, son of Charles and Orpha (Hawley) Hough, married (321) **Kathrine Hawkins**, daughter of _____ and _____ (_____) Hawkins.

References:
1, 6. Robert A. Hawley; West Palm Beach, FL to SHF; 3 Apr 1990. (RGH FG4)

(299) **Lucille Hough**, daughter of Charles and Orpha (Hawley) Hough.

References:
1. Robert A. Hawley; West Palm Beach, FL to SHF; 3 Apr 1990. (RGH FG4)

(300) **Gladys Hough**, daughter of Charles and Orpha (Hawley) Hough, married (322) Ben Lawrence, son of _____ and _____ (_____) Lawrence.

References:
1, 6. Robert A. Hawley; West Palm Beach, FL to SHF; 3 Apr 1990. (RGH FG4)

(302) **Eugene Hawley**, son of Alvro N. and Bessie (Lake) Hawley.

References:
1. Robert A. Hawley; West Palm Beach, FL to SHF; 3 Apr 1990. (RGH FG4)

(303) **Helen Jane Hawley**, daughter of Alvro N. and Bessie (Lake) Hawley.
References:
1. Robert A. Hawley; West Palm Beach, FL to SHF; 3 Apr 1990. (RGH FG4)

(306) **John Joseph Hawley**, Jr., son of John Joseph and Cecelia (Keeffe) Hawley, was born December 9, 1905 in Sioux City, Woodbury County, Iowa, and married June 23, 1926 in Sioux City, Woodbury County, Iowa, (323) **Verne A. McKnight**, daughter of James D. and Nellie (Ferrin) McKnight, who was born November

21, 1905 in Sioux City, Woodbury County, Iowa. John Joseph, Jr., died January 29, 1952 in Cuyahoga Falls, Summit County, Ohio. He was a Salesman. They were of Ft. Wayne, Indiana.[12]

References:

1, 6, 12. Robert A. Hawley; West Palm Beach, FL to SHF; Jul 1989. (RGH BK38)

Children:

324*James Phillip Hawley	b. 7 May 1927	d. 7 May 1927
325*Carol Jeanette Hawley	b. 6 Sep 1928	
326*Jacquelin Elaine Hawley	b. 9 Jun 1930	

(307) **James Hawley**, son of John Joseph and Cecelia (Keeffe) Hawley, was born 1906 in Sioux City, Woodbury County, Iowa. James died 1906 in Sioux City, Woodbury County, Iowa. He was stillborn.[12]

References:

1-2, 4. Robert A. Hawley; West Palm Beach, FL to SHF; Jul 1989. (RGH BK38)

(308) **Jennette Hawley**, daughter of John Joseph and Cecelia (Keeffe) Hawley, was born July 28, 1907 in Sioux City, Woodbury County, Iowa. Jennette died April 30, 1912 in Sioux City, Woodbury County, Iowa.

References:

1-2, 4. Robert A. Hawley; West Palm Beach, FL to SHF; 3 Apr 1990. (RGH FG4)

(309) **Marion Hawley**, daughter of John Joseph and Cecelia (Keeffe) Hawley, was born January 5, 1910 in Sioux City, Woodbury County, Iowa, and married June 2, 1930 in Sioux City, Woodbury County, Iowa, (327) **Clifford Taylor**, son of Frank and Carrie (Griffin) Taylor, who was born September 22, 1908 in Sioux City, Woodbury County, Iowa. Marion died November 4, 1978 in Newport Beach, Orange County, California and was buried in Calvery Cemetery, Sioux City, Woodbury County, Iowa. Clifford died November 29, 1979 in Newport Beach, Orange County, California and was buried in Calvery Cemetery, Sioux City,

Woodbury County, Iowa.

She was a Sales Clerk. They were of Sioux City, Iowa.[12]

References:
1-2, 4, 6-8, 10, 12. Robert A. Hawley; West Palm Beach, FL to SHF; 3 Apr 1990.
(RGH FG4)

Children:

328*Shirley Jean Taylor	b. 27 Mar 1931	
329*Joan Taylor	b. 30 Nov 1938	d. 10 May 1956
330*Nancy Taylor	b. 18 Aug 1938	
331*Marjorie Cecelia Taylor	b. 25 Oct 1939	
332*Roberta Taylor	b. 2 Oct 1941	
333*Susan Margaret Taylor	b. 3 Sep 1943	
334*Kathryn Mary Taylor	b. 28 Aug 1950	

(310) **Robert A. Hawley**, son of John Joseph and Cecelia (Keeffe) Hawley, was born July 27, 1915 in Sioux City, Woodbury County, Iowa, and married May 29, 1941 in Bunkie, Avoyelles Parish, Louisiana, (335) **Agnes Elizabeth Burns**, daughter of Joseph Leo and Mary Magadena [Magdalena] (Geering) Burns, who was born December 24, 1918 in Des Moines, Polk County, Iowa. Robert A. died September 22, 1990 in West Palm Beach, Florida. Agnes Elizabeth died January 29, 1987 in Ormond Beach, Volusia County, Florida and was buried in Queen/Peace Cemetery, Royal Palm Beach, Palm Beach County, Florida.

He was a Salesman of West Palm Beach, Florida. He supplied much of the material in this genealogy. He died suddenly of a heart attack. She was of Daytona Beach Shores, Florida.[12]

References:
1-2, 6-8, 10, 12. Robert A. Hawley; West Palm Beach, FL to SHF; 3 Apr 1990.
(RGH FG4)
1, 4. Robert A. Hawley, Jr.; West Palm Beach, FL to SHF; 9 Oct 1990. (DMH)

Children:

336*Kathleen Hawley	b. 5 Mar 1944
337*James Hawley	b. 5 Feb 1947
338*Michaelene Hawley	b. 16 Jan 1949
339*Robert A. Hawley, Jr.	b. 30 Jun 1951
340*Denise Hawley	b. 17 Nov 1954

(313) **Mary Alice Haggard**, daughter of Everet and Alice (Hawley) Haggard.

References:
1. Robert A. Hawley; West Palm Beach, FL to SHF; 3 Apr 1990. (RGH FG4)

TENTH GENERATION

(317) Andrea Ellis, daughter of Bruce and Florence May, Dr., (Hawley) Ellis, married **(341) Richard Easton**, son of _____ and _____ (_____) Easton.

References:
1, 6. Ruama (Coit) Hawley; Tulsa, OK to SHF 2 Aug 1967. (RGH PN1)

She also married **(342) Clint Dodge**, son of _____ and _____ (_____) Dodge.

References:
1, 6. Ruama (Coit) Hawley; Tulsa, OK to SHF; 2 Aug 1967. (RGH PN1)

(319) Joyce Lyons Hawley, daughter of Paul Frederick and Ruhamah [Ruama] Mather (Coit) Hawley, was born March 6, 1942 in Chicago, Cook County, Illinois, and married **(343) Charles E. Johnson**, son of _____ and _____ (_____) Johnson.

References:
1-2, 6. Ruama (Coit) Hawley; Tulsa, OK to SHF 2 Aug 1967. (RGH PN1)

She also married **(344) Bruce Olsen**, son of _____ and _____ (_____) Olsen.

References:
1, 6. Ruama (Coit) Hawley; Tulsa, OK to SHF 2 Aug 1967. (RGH PN1)

(320) Fred Graham Hawley, II, son of Paul Frederick and Ruhamah [Ruama] Mather (Coit) Hawley, was born August 21, 1945 in Pasadena, Los Angeles County, California.

References:
1-2. Ruama (Coit) Hawley; Tulsa, OK to SHF 2 Aug 1967. (RGH PN1)

(324) James Phillip Hawley, son of John Joseph, Jr., and Verne A.

(McKnight) Hawley, was born May 7, 1927 in Sioux City, Woodbury County, Iowa. James Phillip died May 7, 1927 in Sioux City, Woodbury County, Iowa.

References:
1-2, 4. Robert A. Hawley; West Palm Beach, FL to SHF; 3 Apr 1990. (RGH FG4)

(325) Carol Jeanette Hawley, daughter of John Joseph, Jr., and Verne A. (McKnight) Hawley, was born September 6, 1928 in Sioux City, Woodbury County, Iowa, and married December 30, 1950 in Ft. Wayne, Allen County, Indiana, (345) Thomas James Offerle, son of Anthony J. and Gabrielle (Streiberg) Offerle.

References:
1-2, 6-7. Robert A. Hawley; West Palm Beach, FL to SHF; 3 Apr 1990. (RGH FG4)

Children:

346*John Joseph Offerle	b.	19 Apr 1952
347*Anthony Joseph Offerle		
348*Timothy Scott Offerle	b.	24 Nov 1955
349*Karen Lynn Offerle	b.	10 Sep 1956
350*Thomas Patrick Offerle	b.	20 May 1959
351*Donald Gerard Offerle	b.	2 Jun 1963
352*Susanne Marie Offerle	b.	19 Apr 1964

(326) Jacquelin Elaine Hawley, daughter of John Joseph, Jr., and Verne A. (McKnight) Hawley, was born June 9, 1930 in Sioux City, Woodbury County, Iowa, and married October 10, 1955 in Ft. Wayne, Allen County, Indiana, (353) Jerome Peter Hurtgen, Sr., son of Cecil P. and Isabel (Schroeder) Hurtgen, who was born August 13, 1929 in Milwaukee, Milwaukee County, Wisconsin.

References:
1-2, 6-7. Robert A. Hawley; West Palm Beach, FL to SHF; 3 Apr 1990. (RGH FG4)

Children:

354*Jerome Peter Hurtgen, Jr.	b.	20 Jun 1956
355*Christopher John Hurtgen	b.	23 Jul 1960

(328) Shirley Jean Taylor, daughter of Clifford and Marion (Hawley) Taylor, was born March 27, 1931 in Sioux City,

Woodbury County, Iowa, and married September 27, 1952 in Sioux City, Woodbury County, Iowa, **(356) Daniel J. Smith**, son of _____ and _____ (_____) Smith.

References:
1-2, 6-7. Robert A. Hawley; West Palm Beach, FL to SHF; 3 Apr 1990. (RGH FG4)

(329) Joan Taylor, daughter of Clifford and Marion (Hawley) Taylor, was born November 30, 1938 in Sioux City, Woodbury County, Iowa. Joan
died May 10, 1956 in Akron, Plymouth County, Iowa.

References:
1-2, 4. Robert A. Hawley; West Palm Beach, FL to SHF; 3 Apr 1990. (RGH FG4)

(330) Nancy Taylor, daughter of Clifford and Marion (Hawley) Taylor, was born August 18, 1938 in Sioux City, Woodbury County, Iowa, and married August 4, 1962 in Sioux City, Woodbury County, Iowa, **(357) David M. Smith**, son of _____ and _____ (_____) Smith.

References:
1-2, 6-7. Robert A. Hawley; West Palm Beach, FL to SHF; 3 Apr 1990. (RGH FG4)

(331) Marjorie Cecelia Taylor, daughter of Clifford and Marion (Hawley) Taylor, was born October 25, 1939 in Sioux City, Woodbury County, Iowa, and married March 17, 1961 in Sioux City, Woodbury County, Iowa, **(358)** _____ _____, son of _____ and _____ (_____) _____.

References:
1-2, 6-7. Robert A. Hawley; West Palm Beach, FL to SHF; 3 Apr 1990. (RGH FG4)

(332) Roberta Taylor, daughter of Clifford and Marion (Hawley) Taylor, was born October 2, 1941 in Sioux City, Woodbury County, Iowa, and married August 5, 1965 in Sioux City, Woodbury County, Iowa, **(359)** _____ _____, son of _____ and _____ (_____) _____.

References:
1-2, 6-7. Robert A. Hawley; West Palm Beach, FL to SHF; 3 Apr 1990. (RGH FG4)

(333) Susan Margaret Taylor, daughter of Clifford and Marion (Hawley) Taylor, was born September 3, 1943 in Sioux City, Woodbury County, Iowa, and married August 3, 1963 in Sioux City, Woodbury County, Iowa,

(360) Thomas M. Smith, son of _____ and _____ (_____) Smith.

References:
1. Robert A. Hawley; West Palm Beach, FL to SHF; 3 Apr 1990. (RGH FG4)

(334) Kathryn Mary Taylor, daughter of Clifford and Marion (Hawley) Taylor, was born August 28, 1950 and married **(361) James Rudd**, son of _____ and _____ (_____) Rudd.

References:
1-2, 6. Robert A. Hawley; West Palm Beach, FL to SHF; 3 Apr 1990. (RGH FG4)

(336) Kathleen Hawley, daughter of Robert A. and Agnes Elizabeth (Burns) Hawley, was born March 5, 1944 in Sioux City, Woodbury County, Iowa, and married December 31, 1970 in No. Palm Beach, Palm Beach County, Florida, **(362) Robert V. Romani**, son of Carmen and Daphne T. (Sofia) Romani, who was born August 21, 1945 in White Plains, Westchester County, New York.

He is a Lawyer. They live in West Palm Beach, Florida.[12]

References:
1-2, 6-8, 12. Robert A. Hawley; West Palm Beach, FL to SHF; 3 Apr 1990. (RGH FG4)

Children:

363*Julie Ann Romani	b.	30 Dec 1964
364*Susan Theresa Romani	b.	6 Jul 1974

She also married **(365) Gene Ruggs**, son of _____ and _____ (_____) Ruggs.

References:

1, 6. Robert A. Hawley; West Palm Beach, FL to SHF; 3 Apr 1990. (RGH FG4)

(337) **James Hawley**, son of Robert A. and Agnes Elizabeth (Burns) Hawley, was born February 5, 1947 in Sioux City, Woodbury County, Iowa, and married October 3, 1970 in Washington, DC, (366) **Jill Fitzgerald**, daughter of John W. and Alice (Donovan) Fitzgerald, who was born April 18, 1947 in Washington, DC.
He is a General Manager. They live in Apopka, Florida.[12]

References:

1-2, 6-8, 12. Robert A. Hawley; West Palm Beach, FL to SHF; 3 Apr 1990. (RGH FG4)

Children:

367*James Michael Hawley	b.	8 Jan 1972
368*Jacqueline Hawley	b.	17 Dec 1972
369*Jonathan Andrew Hawley	b.	30 Apr 1989

(338) **Michaelene Hawley**, daughter of Robert A. and Agnes Elizabeth (Burns) Hawley, was born January 16, 1949 in Sioux City, Woodbury County, Iowa.
She is a Missionary Sister, M.S.H.R. of Philadelphia, Pennsylvania.[12]

References:

1-2, 12. Robert A. Hawley; West Palm Beach, FL to SHF; 3 Apr 1990. (RGH FG4)

(339) **Robert A. Hawley**, Jr., son of Robert A. and Agnes Elizabeth (Burns) Hawley, was born June 30, 1951 in Sioux City, Woodbury County, Iowa, and married July 3, 1971 in Lake Worth, Palm Beach County, Florida, (370) **Margaret Matthews**, daughter of Robert C. and Daisy (Rogers) Matthews, who was born June 20, 1950 in South Carolina.
He is a Lawyer. She is a Dental Hygienist. They live in West Palm Beach, Florida.[12]

References:
1-2, 6-8, 12. Robert A. Hawley; West Palm Beach, FL to SHF; 3 Apr 1990. (RGH FG4)

Children:

371*Joseph Hawley	b.	11 Sep 1973
372*Samantha Elizabeth Hawley	b.	15 Apr 1988

(340) **Denise Hawley**, daughter of Robert A. and Agnes Elizabeth (Burns) Hawley, was born November 17, 1954 and married August 17, 1973 in Rockford, Surry County, North Carolina, (373) **Larry Pearce**, son of Dale G. and Shirley J. (Bole) Pearce, who was born October 12, 1953 in Butler, Butler County, Pennsylvania.

She is a Utilities Manager. They live in Deltona, Florida. He was of Atlantis, Florida.[12]

References:
1-2, 6-8, 12. Robert A. Hawley; West Palm Beach, FL to SHF; 3 Apr 1990. (RGH FG4)

Children:

374*Lori Ann Pearce	b.	15 Jan 1975
375*Billy Pearce	b.	16 Apr 1976

ELEVENTH GENERATION

(346) John Joseph Offerle, son of Thomas James and Carol Jeanette (Hawley) Offerle, was born 19 Apr 1952 in Ft. Wayne, Allen County, Indiana, and married June 7, 1975, **(376) Lauren G. Shurr**, daughter of _____ and _____ (_____) Shurr.

References:
1-2, 6-7. Robert A. Hawley; West Palm Beach, FL to SHF; 3 Apr 1990. (RGH FG4)

(347) Anthony Joseph Offerle, son of Thomas James and Carol Jeanette (Hawley) Offerle, married March 21, 1975 in Elgin, Kane County, Illinois, **(377)** _____ _____, daughter of _____ and _____ (_____) _____.

References:
1, 6-7. Robert A. Hawley; West Palm Beach, FL to SHF; Jul 1989. (RGH BK38)

(348) Timothy Scott Offerle, son of Thomas James and Carol Jeanette (Hawley) Offerle, was born November 24, 1955 in Ft. Wayne, Allen County, Indiana, and married May 19, 1979 in Indianapolis, Marion County, Indiana, **(378) Stacy Lee Shew**, daughter of _____ and _____ (_____) Shew.

References:
1-2, 6-7. Robert A. Hawley; West Palm Beach, FL to SHF; 3 Apr 1990. (RGH FG4)

(349) Karen Lynn Offerle, daughter of Thomas James and Carol Jeanette (Hawley) Offerle, was born September 10, 1956 in Ft. Wayne, Allen County, Indiana.

References:
1-2. Robert A. Hawley; West Palm Beach, FL to SHF; 3 Apr 1990. (RGH FG4)

(350) Thomas Patrick Offerle, son of Thomas James and Carol Jeanette (Hawley) Offerle, was born May 20, 1959 in Ft. Wayne, Allen County, Indiana.

References:
1-2. Robert A. Hawley; West Palm Beach, FL to SHF; 3 Apr 1990. (RGH FG4)

(351) Donald Gerard Offerle, son of Thomas James and Carol Jeanette (Hawley) Offerle, was born June 2, 1963 in Ft. Wayne, Allen County, Indiana.

References:
1-2. Robert A. Hawley; West Palm Beach, FL to SHF; 3 Apr 1990. (RGH FG4)

(352) Susanne Marie Offerle, daughter of Thomas James and Carol Jeanette (Hawley) Offerle, was born 19 Apr 1964 in Ft. Wayne, Allen County, Indiana.

References:
1-2. Robert A. Hawley; West Palm Beach, FL to SHF; 3 Apr 1990. (RGH FG4)

(354) Jerome Peter Hurtgen, Jr., son of Jerome Peter, Sr., and Jacquelin Elaine (Hawley) Hurtgen, was born June 20, 1956 in Douglas, Allegan County, Michigan, and married November 15, 1979, **(379) Darcy Schearer**, daughter of _____ and _____ (_____) Schearer.

References:
1-2, 6-7. Robert A. Hawley; West Palm Beach, FL to SHF; 3 Apr 1990. (RGH FG4)

(355) Christopher John Hurtgen, son of Jerome Peter, Sr., and Jacquelin Elaine (Hawley) Hurtgen, was born July 23, 1960 in Holland, Ottawa County, Michigan.

References:
1-2. Robert A. Hawley; West Palm Beach, FL to SHF; 3 Apr 1990. (RGH FG4)

(363) Julie Ann Romani, daughter of Robert V. and Kathleen (Hawley) Romani, was born December 30, 1964 in Omaha, Douglas County, Nebraska, and married February 3, 1984 in West Palm Beach, Palm Beach County, Florida, **(380) Jimmy Frady**, son of _____ and _____ (_____) Frady.

References:
1-2, 6-7. Robert A. Hawley; West Palm Beach, FL to SHF; 3 Apr 1990. (RGH FG4)

(364) Susan Theresa Romani, daughter of Robert V. and Kathleen (Hawley) Romani, was born July 6, 1974.

References:
1-2. Robert A. Hawley; West Palm Beach, FL to SHF; 3 Apr 1990. (RGH FG4)

(367) James Michael Hawley, son of James and Jill (Fitzgerald) Hawley, was born January 8, 1972 in West Palm Beach, Palm Beach County, Florida.

References:
1-2. Robert A. Hawley; West Palm Beach, FL to SHF; 3 Apr 1990. (RGH FG4)

(368) Jacqueline Hawley, daughter of James and Jill (Fitzgerald) Hawley, was born December 17, 1972 in West Palm Beach, Palm Beach County, Florida.

References:
1-2. Robert A. Hawley; West Palm Beach, FL to SHF; 3 Apr 1990. (RGH FG4)

(369) Jonathan Andrew Hawley, son of James and Jill (Fitzgerald) Hawley, was born 30 Apr 1989 in Orlando, Orange County, Florida.

References:
1-2. Robert A. Hawley; West Palm Beach, FL to SHF; 3 Apr 1990. (RGH FG4)

(371) Joseph Hawley, son of Robert A., Jr., and Margaret (Matthews) Hawley, was born September 11, 1973 in West Palm Beach, Palm Beach County, Florida.

References:
1-2. Robert A. Hawley; West Palm Beach, FL to SHF; 3 Apr 1990. (RGH FG4)

(372) **Samantha Elizabeth Hawley**, daughter of Robert A., Jr., and Margaret (Matthews) Hawley, was born 15 Apr 1988 in West Palm Beach, Palm Beach County, Florida.

References:
1-2. Robert A. Hawley; West Palm Beach, FL to SHF; 3 Apr 1990. (RGH FG4)

(374) **Lori Ann Pearce**, daughter of Larry and Denise (Hawley) Pearce, was born January 15, 1975 in Raeford, Hoak County, North Carolina.

References:
1-2. Robert A. Hawley; West Palm Beach, FL to SHF; 3 Apr 1990. (RGH FG4)

(375) **Billy Pearce**, son of Larry and Denise (Hawley) Pearce, was born 16 Apr 1976 in Raeford, Hoak County, North Carolina.

References:
1-2. Robert A. Hawley; West Palm Beach, FL to SHF; 3 Apr 1990. (RGH FG4)

Name	Serial No.	Born /Chr	Died /Bur	Spouse or *Father Name
Crosser, _____	.274	___	___	_____ _____
Crosser, Martin.	.274	___	___	Josephine Hawley
Davis, Agnes	46	1745	1818	Joseph Hawley
Davis, Elisha.	80	___	___	Susanna Hawley
Davis, Evan.	46	___	___	Susanna Jones
Davis, Mary.	.122	1791	1869	Benjamin Hawley
Davis, Samuel.	.122	___	___	Mary _____
Davis, _____	80	___	___	_____ _____
Dodge, _____	.342	___	___	_____ _____
Dodge, Clint	.342	___	___	Andrea Ellis
Donovan, Alice	.366	___	___	John W. Fitzgerald
Easton, _____	.341	___	___	_____ _____
Easton, Richard.	.341	___	___	Andrea Ellis
Eavenson, _____	49	___	___	_____ _____
Eavenson, Elizabeth.	49	___	___	William Hawley
Ellis, Andrea.	.317	___	___	Richard Easton
Ellis, Bruce	.316	___	___	Florence May Hawley Dr.
Ellis, _____	.316	___	___	_____ _____
Eveson, _____	.101	___	___	_____ _____
Eveson, Hannah	.101	___	___	Nathan Hawley
Farrar, _____	.266	___	___	_____ _____
Farrar, Louise	.266	___	___	James Graham Hawley
Ferrin, Nellie	.323	___	___	James D. McKnight
Fitzgerald, Jill	.366	1947	___	James Hawley
Fitzgerald, John W..	.366	___	___	Alice Donovan
Frady, _____	.380	___	___	_____ _____
Frady, Jimmy	.380	___	___	Julie Ann Romani
Frame, _____	48	___	___	_____ _____
Frame, Hannah.	48	___	___	William Hawley
Frank, _____	.314	___	___	_____ _____
Frank, Ben	.314	___	___	Alice Hawley
Furnesss, _____	.177	___	___	_____ _____
Furness, Oliver.	.177	___	___	Ann Kent
Gabiter, Dinah	13	1698	1761	Benjamin Hawley
Gabiter, John.	13	___	___	_____ _____
Geering, Mary Magadena	.335	1881	1948	Joseph Leo Burns
Grewell, Alice	.198	1821	1897	Joseph Hawley
Grewell, Timothy	.198	___	1850	Alice [Pinnock] Pennock
Griffin, Carrie.	.327	___	___	Frank Taylor
Haggard, _____	.312	___	___	_____ _____
Haggard, Everet.	.312	___	___	Alice Hawley
Haggard, Mary Alice.	.313	___	___	*Everet Haggard
Hawkins, _____	.321	___	___	_____ _____
Hawkins, Kathrine.	.321	___	___	Elvin Hough
Hawley, _____	.1	___	___	_____ _____
Hawley, _____	98	___	___	*Albert Hawley
Hawley, _____	99	___	___	*Albert Hawley
Hawley, _____	.237	___	___	*Albert Hawley
Hawley, _____	.238	___	___	*Lewis Hawley
Hawley, _____	.239	___	___	*Lewis Hawley
Hawley, _____	.241	___	___	*Joseph Hawley Jr.
Hawley, _____	.242	___	___	*Joseph Hawley Jr.

Name	Serial No.	Born /Chr	Died /Bur	Spouse or *Father Name
Hawley, Enos 75		1799	____	Mary S. _____
Hawley, Esther 38		1763	1816	Daniel Kent
Hawley, Eugene 302		____	____	*Alvro N. Hawley
Hawley, Florence May, Dr.. .292		1906	____	Bruce Ellis
Hawley, Francis. 7		____	____	*Thomas Hawley
Hawley, Francis [Frank] M. .191		1853	____	Bell C. Adams
Hawley, Frank Lawrence . . .272		1886	1950	*Cicero Stoner Hawley
Hawley, Fred Graham. 269		1874	1962	Amy May Roach
Hawley, Fred Graham, II. . .320		1945	____	*Paul Frederick Hawley
Hawley, Gertrude R.. 160		____	____	_____
Hawley, Gideon 72		____	____	*Robert Hawley
Hawley, Hannah 27		1766	____	*Benjamin Hawley Jr.
Hawley, Hannah 77		____	____	*Robert Hawley
Hawley, Hannah 63		1804	1880	*Caleb Hawley
Hawley, Hannah Mary. 150		1834	____	_____
Hawley, Harriet. 168		1823	____	*Enos Hawley
Hawley, Helen Jane 303		____	____	*Alvro N. Hawley
Hawley, Helen Margaret . . .273		1890	1895	Newel H. Wadsworth
Hawley, Henry C. 127		1849	____	*Benjamin Hawley
Hawley, Irvin. 221		____	____	*Richard Hawley
Hawley, Isaac. 199		1841	____	*Joseph Hawley
Hawley, Issac. 44		1775	1837	*Joseph Hawley
Hawley, Jacquelin Elaine . .326		1930	____	Jerome Peter Hurtgen Sr.
Hawley, Jacqueline 368		1972	____	*James Hawley
Hawley, James. 307		1906	1906	*John Joseph Hawley
Hawley, James. 337		1947	____	Jill Fitzgerald
Hawley, James Dobbins. . . .264		1863	____	*Robert Hawley
Hawley, James G. 117		1825	1917	Mary B. Bishop
Hawley, James Graham 183		1836	____	Louise Farrar
Hawley, James Melville . . .209		1870	____	*James G. Hawley
Hawley, James Michael. . . .367		1972	____	*James Hawley
Hawley, James Phillip. . . .324		1927	1927	*John Joseph Hawley Jr.
Hawley, Jane 111		1826	____	Caleb Windle
Hawley, Jennette 308		1907	1912	*John Joseph Hawley
Hawley, Jesse. 107		1816	____	Adeline Windle
Hawley, Jesse. 69		1806	1887	Esther T. Meredith
Hawley, Jesse. 143		1836	____	*Simon Hawley
Hawley, Jesse D. 158		____	____	_____
Hawley, Jessie 60		1796	1880	Eliza Brown
Hawley, Joel 68		1804	____	Catharine B. Williamson
Hawley, John 19		1743	____	*Benjamin Hawley
Hawley, John 147		1778	1814	*Joseph Hawleyp
Hawley, John 45		1839	____	*Benjamin Hawley
Hawley, John Joseph. 285		1883	1940	Cecelia Keeffe
Hawley, John Joseph, Jr. . .306		1905	1952	Verne A. McKnight
Hawley, Jonathan Andrew. . .369		1989	____	*James Hawley
Hawley, Joseph 10		1973	____	*Robert A. Hawley Jr.
Hawley, Joseph 16		____	____	*Thomas Hawley
Hawley, Joseph 24		1735	1817	Elizabeth Spackman
Hawley, Joseph 114		1848	____	*Calib Hawley
Hawley, Joseph 139		1760	1856	Rebecca Meredith
Hawley, Joseph 155		1818	1905	Alice Grewell

Name	Serial No.	Born /Chr	Died /Bur	Spouse or *Father Name
Hawley, Samantha Elizabeth	.372	1988	___	*Robert A. Hawley Jr.
Hawley, Samuel Davis	.125	1830	___	Susan Altemus
Hawley, Samuel W.	.152	1840	___	*Joel Hawley
Hawley, Sarah.	.9	___	___	*Thomas Hawley
Hawley, Sarah.	.120	1833	1895	*Caleb Hawley Jr.
Hawley, Sarah.	.203	1848	___	*Joseph Hawley
Hawley, Sarah.	.124	1828	___	Robert B. Hiddleson
Hawley, Sarah.	.134	1832	1832	*Jessie Hawley
Hawley, Simon.	66	1801	1863	___ ___
Hawley, Susanna.	.8	___	___	*Thomas Hawley
Hawley, Susanna.	30	1770	___	Elisha Davis
Hawley, Susannah [Susan]	18	1740	1770	Christopher Nupher
Hawley, Tamer.	31	1772	___	Joshua Hicklin
Hawley, Theordore.	.220	___	___	*Richard Hawley
Hawley, Thomas	.1	1654	1717	Francis [Maling] Malin
Hawley, Thomas	.3	___	___	*Thomas Hawley
Hawley, Thomas	23	1758	1781	*Benjamin Hawley Jr.
Hawley, Thomas	62	1802	___	*Caleb Hawley
Hawley, Thomas "again"	.5	___	___	*Thomas Hawley
Hawley, Thomas "2nd again"	11	___	___	*Thomas Hawley
Hawley, Thomas Leonard, Capt.	84	1838	___	*Calib Hawley
Hawley, Thomas P.	.207	1854	___	*James G. Hawley
Hawley, Walter Eastman	.271	1881	___	Edith Trout
Hawley, William.	17	1737	1826	Hannah Taylor
Hawley, William.	.202	1847	1897	*Joseph Hawley
Hawley, William.	.126	1833	___	*Benjamin Hawley
Hawley, William.	40	1766	1836	Ann Marshall
Hawley, William B.	.208	1857	___	*James G. Hawley
Hawley, William Enos	.263	1860	___	*Robert Hawley
Hays, ___	.280	___	___	___ ___
Hays, John Byron	.280	___	___	Eldora Hawley
Heston, ___	.195	___	___	___ ___
Heston, Elizabeth [Hester]	.195	___	___	Benjamin Hawley
Hewes, Anna Margaret	.290	1867	___	David Jones Reinhardt
Hewes, Thomas.	.290	___	___	Elizabeth Andrews Miller
Hicklin, ___	81	___	___	___ ___
Hicklin, ___	84	___	___	___ ___
Hicklin, Hannah.	82	___	___	Joseph Marshall
Hicklin, Jesse	83	___	___	___ ___
Hicklin, John.	84	___	___	Dinah Hawley
Hicklin, Joshua.	81	___	___	Tamer Hawley
Hiddleson, Robert B.	.215	___	1858	Sarah Hawley
Hill, Stella Jane.	.275	___	___	Nathan C. Hawley
Hillborn, ___	20	___	___	___ ___
Hillborn, Catharine.	20	1696	1789	Benjamin Hawley
Hoffman, Elizabeth	.282	1830	1915	John W. Bell
Hole, David.	.121	___	___	Anna ___
Hole, Tacy	.121	___	___	Caleb Hawley Jr.
Hoopes, ___	50	___	___	___ ___
Hoopes, ___	85	___	___	___ ___
Hoopes, Deborah.	85	___	___	Benjamin Hawley
Hoopes, Phebe.	50	___	___	William Hawley

Name	Serial No.	Born /Chr	Died /Bur	Spouse or *Father Name
Maudlin, Bertha.	231	___	___	*Thomas Maudlin
Maudlin, Ella.	223	___	___	*Thomas Maudlin
Maudlin, Jesse	228	___	___	*Thomas Maudlin
Maudlin, Lucinda	229	___	___	*Thomas Maudlin
Maudlin, Mary.	225	___	___	*Thomas Maudlin
Maudlin, Rethia.	230	___	___	William Risdom
Maudlin, Sylvester	224	___	___	*Thomas Maudlin
Maudlin, Thomas.	222	___	___	Elvira Hawley
Maudlin, Thomas.	226	___	___	*Thomas Maudlin
McBride, Mary Ann.	181	___	___	Edward [Emanuel] Hawley
McCann, _____.	78	___	___	
McCann, Arthur	78	___	___	Rachel Hawley
McDonald, _____.	278	___	___	
McDonald, Margaret	278	___	___	Francis [Frank] M Hawley
McKnight, James D.	323	___	___	Nellie Ferrin
McKnight, Verne A.	323	1905	___	John Joseph Hawley Jr.
Mendenhall, Ann.	153	___	___	John Meredith
Meredith, Esther T..	153	1807	1900	Jesse Hawley
Meredith, John	153	___	___	Ann Mendenhall
Meredith, Rebecca.	64	1766	1851	Joseph Hawley
Meredith, Simon.	64	___	___	Dinah Pugh
Miller, _____.	304	___	___	
Miller, Elizabeth Andrews.	290	___	___	Thomas Hewes
Miller, Opal	304	___	___	Alvro N. Hawley
Moore, _____.	165	___	___	
Moore, _____.	166	___	___	*Charles Moore
Moore, _____.	161	___	___	*Charles Moore
Moore, Charles	161	___	1890	Dinah Hawley
Moore, Henry J..	162	___	___	*Charles Moore
Moore, James M..	164	___	___	*Charles Moore
Moore, Richard	163	___	___	*Charles Moore
Morse, Mary.	291	___	___	David Llewellyn Roach
Neary, _____.	315	___	___	
Neary, _____.	315	___	___	Edna Risdom
Nupher, _____.	51	___	___	
Nupher, Christopher.	51	___	___	Susannah [Susan] Hawley
Nutter, Sadie Emmeline	318	___	___	Ruel Harlan Coit
Offerle, Anthony J..	345	___	___	Gabrielle Streiberg
Offerle, Anthony Joseph.	347	___	___	*Thomas James Offerle
Offerle, Donald Gerard	351	1963	___	*Thomas James Offerle
Offerle, John Joseph	346	1952	___	Lauren G. Shurr
Offerle, Karen Lynn.	349	1956	___	*Thomas James Offerle
Offerle, Susanne Marie	352	1964	___	*Thomas James Offerle
Offerle, Thomas James.	345	___	___	Carol Jeanette Hawley
Offerle, Thomas Patrick.	350	1959	___	*Thomas James Offerle
Offerle, Timothy Scott	348	1955	___	Stacy Lee Shew
Olsen, _____.	344	___	___	
Olsen, Bruce	344	___	___	Joyce Lyons Hawley
Paxson, Benjamin	129	___	___	Ruth _____
Paxson, Rachael.	129	___	___	Richard Hawley
Pearce, Billy.	375	1976	___	*Larry Pearce
Pearce, Dale G..	373	___	___	Shirley J. Bole

Name	Serial No.	Born /Chr	Died /Bur	Spouse or *Father Name
Taylor, Frank.	327	___	___	Carrie Griffin
Taylor, Hannah	47	___	___	William Hawley
Taylor, Joan	329	1938	1956	*Clifford Taylor
Taylor, Kathryn Mary . . .	334	1950	___	James Rudd
Taylor, Marjorie Cecelia . .	331	1939	___	
Taylor, Nancy.	330	1938	___	David M. Smith
Taylor, Roberta.	332	1941	___	
Taylor, Shirley Jean . . .	328	1931	___	Daniel J. Smith
Taylor, Susan Margaret . . .	333	1943	___	Thomas M. Smith
Thomas, _____.	211	___	___	*Isaac G. Thomas
Thomas, _____.	212	___	___	*Isaac G. Thomas
Thomas, _____.	213	___	___	*Isaac G. Thomas
Thomas, _____.	214	___	___	*Isaac G. Thomas
Thomas, _____.	210	___	___	
Thomas, Isaac G.	210	___	___	Eliza Hawley
Trout, _____	295	___	___	
Trout, Edith	295	___	___	Walter Eastman Hawley
Wadsworth, _____	296	___	___	
Wadsworth, Newel H.. . . .	296	___	___	Helen Margaret Hawley
Warrington, _____.	112	___	___	
Warrington, Mary	112	___	___	Amos Hawley
Weyenburg, _____	311	___	___	
Weyenburg, Ruth.	311	___	___	John Joseph Hawley
Wherry, _____.	217	___	___	
Wherry, Elijah	217	___	___	Ella Hawley
Wherry, Julian	218	___	___	*Elijah Wherry
Whitaker, _____	294	___	___	
Whitaker, Forrest M. . . .	294	___	___	Agnes Genevieve Hawley
Willets, _____	265	___	___	
Willets, Rachel L.	265	___	___	Alfred Hawley
Williamson, _____. . . .	149	___	___	
Williamson, Catharine B. . .	149	___	___	Joel Hawley
Windle, _____.	193	___	___	
Windle, _____.	197	___	___	
Windle, Adeline.	193	___	___	Jesse Hawley
Windle, Caleb.	197	___	___	Jane Hawley
Woodward, _____	96	___	___	
Woodward, _____.	97	___	___	
Woodward, Ann.	175	1795	1844	William Kent
Woodward, Elizabeth. . . .	97	___	___	Joseph Hawley Jr.
Woodward, Richard.	96	___	___	Elizabeth Hawley
Woodward, Thomas	175	___	___	Mary _____
Yearsley, Patience	71	___	1828	Robert Hawley
Yearsley, Thomas	71	___	___	

www.ingramcontent.com/pod-product-compliance
Lightning Source LLC
Chambersburg PA
CBHW072205270326
41930CB00011B/2537